THE
QUOTABLE
WILL ★ ★
★ ★
ROGERS

THE
QUOTABLE
WILL
ROGERS

BY JOSEPH H. CARTER

Photographs by Will Rogers Memorial Commission Archives

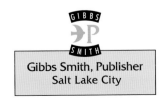

Gibbs Smith, Publisher
Salt Lake City

First Edition
09 08 07 06   5 4 3 2

Text © 2005 Joseph H. Carter
Photographs © 2005 Will Rogers Memorial Commission Archives
Illustrations © 2005 Charles Banks Wilson

Published by
Gibbs Smith, Publisher
P.O. Box 667
Layton, Utah 84041

Orders: 1.800.748.5439
www.gibbs-smith.com

Designed by Martin Yeeles

Printed and bound in Hong Kong

Library of Congress Cataloging-in-Publication Data
Carter, Joseph H.
The quotable Will Rogers / Joseph H. Carter. — 1st ed.
p. cm.
ISBN 1-58685-696-0
1. Rogers, Will, 1879-1935.
2. Rogers, Will, 1879-1935 — Quotations.
3. Entertainers — United States — Biography.
4. Humorists,
American — Biography.
I. Rogers, Will, 1879-1935. II. Title.

PN2287.R74C344 2006
792.702'8'092 — dc22

2005024770

To my wife, Michelle.

FOREWORD

I ain't gonna lie to you. Usually when somebody tells you that, it means they are about to lie like a dog. Well, here's the truth.

Joe Carter knows more about the late great Will Rogers than anybody else in the known world and parts of Oklahoma. (Speakin' of Oklahoma, my grandmother was a half-Cherokee woman born in or around Broken Bow back in 1906, so that means I have some good Cherokee blood in me too . . . just like Ol' Will.)

I'm happy about that, by the way. I'm also happy to be Joe Carter's friend and that he's mine. He's a great spirit, a great writer and a great Oklahoman. And it means I'll get a free copy of his new book on my great hero, Will Rogers.

I've been blessed that I got to play the part of Will Rogers on Broadway in *The Will Rogers Follies.* And all I can say is that it made me a better person. Unlike Ol' Will, I've met a few people I didn't like (and vice versa). But after playing Will, it doesn't happen as often and I get over it quicker.

Thanks, Will, and thank you, Joe Carter, for another great book on Oklahoma's foremost native son, Will Rogers.

Larry Gatlin

PREFACE

Alive, Will Rogers was phenomenally successful. Longer than he lived, Will Rogers remained Americana personified. He wrote six books during his fifty-five years. Following his 1935 death, more than 235 titles had been written about him. Will Rogers starred in seventy-one motion pictures. Fifteen years following his death, his own saga, *The Story of Will Rogers,* became a major cinema hit.

During the 1920s, Will Rogers was a comic in New York's glittery *Ziegfeld Follies.* Seventy years later, his life was set to music on Broadway, where *The Will Rogers Follies: A Life in Revue* won six Tony Awards. During two decades as a syndicated columnist, he wrote four thousand articles that were widely quoted at the time. Over the next seven decades, scores of columnists regularly quoted his savvy notions, ideas and cowboy humor.

Will Rogers was America's pioneer radio commentator. Seldom personal, he equally taunted both Democrats and Republicans. Contrasting twenty-first-century pundits and commentators, he tempered criticism with warm wit devoid of malice.

During Hollywood's early racy era, scandals, divorces and love trysts among actors were common headlines. Superstar Will Rogers remained the faithful husband, adored father and dedicated family man at home on the ranch. Born into a mixed-blood Cherokee ranch family on the wild frontier, Will Rogers was an accomplished nineteenth-century cowboy, fancy trick roper and horseman well before automobiles were invented.

In the twenty-first century, he was formally named fortieth among the most influential fathers of aviation. Most often traveling by steamship, Will circumnavigated the globe three times. He died in a single-engine airplane crash at the northernmost point of America while preparing for the world's first transpolar flight. Networks were silenced for thirty minutes observing his death. Planes towing black banners flew over New York. More than fifty thousand people marched past his bier. His statue was mounted in the nation's capitol so that he could "keep an eye on Congress."

Here was a man who was born on the rugged American frontier in a log house devoid of radio, electric lightbulbs, indoor toilets and water faucets. Yet, Will had cannily mastered all the communication media that had burst upon civilization during his ensuing fifty-five years.

Along the way, he captured the hearts of so many Americans.

ACKNOWLEDGMENTS

Senator Stratton Taylor, Will Rogers' most dedicated supporter; Steven K. Gragert, archivist-historian; Pat Lowe, librarian; Rick Mobley, graphic designer; Hollie Keith, editor; and Michelle Lefebvre-Carter, director, Will Rogers Memorial Commission of Oklahoma.

> I WAS BORN ON NOV. 4, WHICH IS ELECTION DAY... MY BIRTHDAY HAS MADE MORE MEN AND SENT MORE BACK TO HONEST WORK THAN ANY OTHER DAYS IN THE YEAR.

Clem Rogers was a cattleman, Cherokee, judge, senator, banker, businessman and eldest delegate to the Oklahoma Constitutional Convention of 1907.

The only known photo of Mary America Schrimsher Rogers reflects her quarter-blood Cherokee heritage. She was a refined churchwoman, frontier pioneer, war refugee, first lady of her husband's sprawling ranch and the mother of eight, including Will Rogers.

ALL ABOUT WILL

Election day, November 4, 1879, in the southeast corner room of a log-walled, colonial-style seven-room house, Mary America Schrimsher Rogers gave birth to the son of Clement Vann Rogers, their eighth and final child.

Clement Vann Rogers and Mary America Schrimsher met while attending a boarding school in the Cherokee Nation capital of Tahlequah. Mary loved her studies, was refined, musically gifted and a Methodist. Clem despised school, was a hard-riding cattleman and commercially astute. They married and moved to his Cooweescoowee District ranch two years before the Civil War started.

The proud father dubbed the newborn Colonel William Penn Adair Rogers, as a salute to the Indian military leader who was his battalion commander during the terrible War Between the States. The Civil War that had ended fourteen years earlier had left stains of blood across the Cherokee Nation, where Indian clans and even cousins fought each other in a senseless battle fifteen hundred miles away.

Men of the Cherokee Nation, including cavalry captain Clem Rogers, fought four years with the South under the famous Colonel Adair. They rampaged across Arkansas and parts of Indian Territory that would become Oklahoma in 1907.

Here is the 1870s birthplace home of Will Rogers, with Texas longhorn cattle grazing on the 400-acre ranch near Oologah, Oklahoma. The house was built of logs with clapboard siding added later, and the home was dubbed "the White House on the Verdigris River." Fully restored, the living-history ranch is open every day of the year.

On the day of Will Rogers' birth, the fighting had passed and much of the remaining animosity and revenge had cooled. Mary and Clem Rogers had abandoned their original and embattled homestead and trading post when the war erupted. Clem had joined the mounted cavalry to battle hostile forces who demolished their holdings. Mary had ridden horseback for eighty miles through freezing rain to gain safety. She and a freed slave galloped side by side, cuddling her first-born daughter, who then died from the exposure. As Clem endured combat, Mary, along with her family, was forced to flee to wooded areas near Bonham, Texas, to encamp beyond harm's way during the war.

YOU CAN BE KILLED JUST AS DEAD IN AN UNJUSTI-FIED WAR AS YOU CAN IN ONE PROTECTING YOUR OWN HOME.

From 1865 until 1870, the Rogers family had managed to scrape together ample funds to return to the range they had abandoned nearly a decade earlier. Part Cherokee, Clem paid $25 to Tom Boot, a full-blood Indian, to regain rights to the range. Using hand-hewed logs of walnut, oak and pecan trees squared at twelve inches, he built the home one 24-by-24-foot square room at a time. First built was the master bedroom where Will Rogers was born. Allowing a sixteen-foot fire break called a "dog trot," the second log room was located next to the first one and squared off. The space between was enclosed later and became a hallway.

In a second-story venture, two rooms and a large walk-in closet arose over the two original boxes for upstairs bedrooms, with a southern-exposure porch added at ground level and an open sleeping area above.

A kitchen, dining area and guest bedroom were tacked onto the north side of the log walls. A path led to an outhouse, and pots were placed under beds for nocturnal relief. A cistern that captured rainwater from the roof provided sustenance for the family.

Open fireplaces serviced each of the four log rooms, while a massive cooking stove warmed the kitchen and a potbellied woodstove served the eating area. Protected

This oil-on-canvas painting by Wayne Cooper portrays Will Rogers herding horses at his birthplace ranch. Cooper painted the face of Joe Carter, author of this book, on the white horse in the background. Freed slave Dan Walker, who taught Will Rogers how to rope, is also depicted as a cowboy.

from north winds by a hill, the house faced a mile-wide valley that reached toward the Verdigris River. Under Cherokee law, God owned the land but Clem had full rights to use the lush grasses across a V-shaped domain fenced by the Verdigris River to the east and the Caney River to the west, running a dozen miles north from where the streams converged.

Though he had little formal education, Clem Rogers was astute in Cherokee governmental affairs that provided free land. He also had mastered farming, ranching and commerce through tough trials and hard experience, which added to his native intelligence.

Native bluestem, with roots curling twelve feet deep, begat the name "Tall Grass Prairie." Prime food for live-stock and wildlife abounded. On the negative side, when lightning struck, dry grasses fed wildfires that raged for miles. The deep water-tapping roots of the bluestem quickly regenerated the pastures.

AMERICA IS A LAND OF OPPORTUNITY AND DON'T EVER FORGET IT.

The land labeled Indian Territory had been assigned by invading Europeans to the five civilized native tribes and

A 1929 Fox production of *They Had to See Paris* starred Will Rogers as an Oklahoma garage owner who struck it rich in oil. His wife, played by Irene Rich, insisted that they move to Europe. Censors of the day struck out parts of the movie, which was somewhat saucy for its time and featured vaudeville dancer Fifi D'Orsay as "the naughty French girl."

A MAN LEARNS BY TWO THINGS. ONE IS READING. THE OTHER IS ASSOCIATING WITH SMARTER PEOPLE.

bands of Plains Indians. While fertile, it was a hostile meeting place of three major air masses: one brought cold from the north; another brought moisture from the Gulf of Mexico; and the last brought fronts that moved eastward from the Pacific Ocean. This bred dangerous, destructive tornados that struck mostly during the springtime. The seasons brought incredibly cold and windy winters and extremely hot summers divided by pleasant springs and autumns. Good water in the rivers that flowed from Kansas nourished native grasses and fertile valleys enriched by silt from floods, creating a perfect setting for ranching and farming.

Following the Civil War, Clem Rogers purchased Texas longhorn cattle for $1 each from near the Gulf of Mexico. He drove the herds northward to his ranch, and then fattened them on the lush bluestem grasses and planted grains. A year following the herd's arrival, the cattle were cautiously driven forty miles northward, sold for $40 a head at Coffeyville, Kansas, and then shipped by rail to hungry families of the East, where men and livestock had been depleted by the terrible war.

Business was good (an investment of a buck plus another dollar of labor costs yielded $40). The family enjoyed frontier riches by the time Will Rogers was born. Clapboard siding had been added to the regal house and painted

The 1935 Fox feature *Life Begins at 40* starred Will Rogers as Kenesaw H. Clark. Sterling Holloway is pictured with the star. *Courtesy of Gordon Kuntz collection.*

white. By 1879, the family home and headquarters of the sprawling ranch had become known as "the White House on the Verdigris." With a huge barn for fine horses and cottages for cowboys' families, the house was the only sign of civilization for miles around. It quickly became a center for hospitality, socializing, government meetings, court hearings, weddings, funerals, dances and religious worship. Travelers were welcomed to eat free delicious meals and to share two full-size beds. Wealth had made fine, imported furniture and even a piano part of the home by 1879.

The Cherokee Nation had appointed Clem Rogers as a judge, who furnished his own courtroom. By the time of Will Rogers' birth, his father had been elected senator, representing the Cooweescoowee District of the Cherokee legislature that met in faraway Tahlequah.

As newlywed twenty-year-olds, Mary and Clem had ventured west to build their future with a cattle ranch and store, and to trade with Osage Indians who had waged war with the Cherokees a few years earlier. Inheriting two

TEN MEN IN THE COUNTRY COULD BUY THE WORLD
AND TEN MILLION CAN'T BUY ENOUGH TO EAT.

Irene Rich played Will Rogers' "reel" wife, Mrs. Pike Peters, in the 1929 Fox production of *They Had to See Paris*.

black slaves, two dozen cows and four horses, their dream was shattered by the Civil War and then rejuvenated richly after peace returned. Clem treated his slaves as free men, business partners, employees or trusted allies. Following the war, the black men and their families — with full membership in the Cherokee Nation — settled on the western edge of the ranch land by the Caney River. Rabb's Creek was named to honor one of the two black brothers; the other brother's name was Houston, just like hero General Sam Houston, the neighbor who had freed Texas from Mexico's domination.

C. V. Rogers, as Clem advertised himself, established headquarters seven miles east of the ex-slaves' homes and within sight of the Verdigris River. Only tall grass divided the enterprises until, years later, railroad tracks were laid squarely in the middle and a village named Oologah was formed around a station.

Baby Will Rogers arrived when Mary and Clem were in their forties. Clem quickly had the boy on a horse. A black cowboy, Dan Walker, was teaching him the rudiments of lariat handling. The lasso was the main tool of herdsmen, necessary to catch calves or fetch animals trapped in a muddy bog. Walker was a first-class cattleman and a skilled roper.

The new city of Beverly Hills anointed Will Rogers as its honorary mayor.

The numerous children of Houston Rogers and his wife, Rabbit, would become Will's main playmates. Cowboys were recruited from Cherokee families to join in the hard labor of cattle raising and farming, and they brought their Indian children to join the happy community.

Aboard ship, Will Rogers and his son Will Jr. en route to Europe, 1925.

With three older daughters and ranch-hand wives to manage the grueling housework, Mary Rogers devoted long hours to her final son. She had lost three children at childbirth. When Will was age three, his sixteen-year-old brother, Robert, died of typhoid. Little Willie, the family's sole male heir, was schooled on his mother's lap. She taught him reading, writing, simple arithmetic and proper diction. Will failed to inherit her fine musical skills but would sing regardless.

Young Willie, who was 9/32 Cherokee, inherited his mother's rich wit and sense of mirth, which was legendary among the Native Americans. In the pre-Columbian era, women served as Cherokee judges and

Will Rogers as a dapper young man.

punished the guiltiest parties with banishment, teasing, laughter and perhaps execution. There was no means of incarceration. Humiliation was worse.

Will's mother, Mary Schrimsher, was the granddaughter of Catherine, the Cherokees' Paint Clan princess who married Welsh immigrant John Gunter. Catherine and John founded the town of Guntersville, Alabama, which was located on the Great Bend of the Tennessee River. Their half-blood Cherokee daughter Elizabeth Hunt Gunter (1804–1877) married Martin Mathew Schrimsher (1806–1865), a full-blood Dutchman. The Schrimshers settled near Tahlequah in Cherokee Nation West, which later became Oklahoma. Well financed by her parents, they were "old settlers" who had moved a few years before President Andrew Jackson forced the migration of about five thousand Cherokees in a deadly bayonet-enforced march dubbed the Trail of Tears. Mary America Schrimsher (1839–1890), who was 1/4 Cherokee of the Paint Clan, was born on a plantation near Tahlequah.

Will's great-grandfather Robert Rogers Sr. was 5/16 Cherokee of the Wolf Clan. Robert, of Irish-Scotch blood, had married a half-blood Cherokee, Lucy Cordery. Born in Georgia, their quarter-blood son, Robert Rogers Jr. (1815–1842), married Sallie Vann (1818–1882), who was 1/2 Cherokee.

Photos of Will Rogers' military school days.

Robert Rogers Jr. was suspected of signing the controversial 1835 Treaty of New Echota in Georgia. Many full-blood Cherokees, including Chief John Ross, denounced and defied the treaty. Under it, the United States government gave five million dollars to Cherokees, provided they relinquished their eastern land claims and moved west to special land in what would become Oklahoma. The treaty truly bears the signature of a Robert Rogers. While stricken with blood poisoning and very ill, a Dr. Robert Rogers of Georgia wrote in his final will and testament that he had signed the treaty. The frontier was raw and law enforcement was spotted. Other signers of the disputed treaty were assassinated, including mostly more mature and older tribal leaders.

Even now, many Cherokee elders disbelieved that Will's grandfather was innocent of signing the hated treaty. The state of Oklahoma's official historical markers near his home on State Highway 59 north of Stilwell credit him with signing the treaty and claims that he was assassinated in revenge.

After the treaty was signed, many Cherokees quietly moved west and became known as "old settlers." Those who later were forced westward by President Jackson's

WE DON'T HAVE TO WORRY ABOUT ANYTHING. NO NATION IN THE HISTORY OF THE WORLD WAS EVER SITTING AS PRETTY. IF WE WANT ANYTHING, ALL WE HAVE TO DO IS GO AND BUY IT ON CREDIT.

army, including Chief John Ross and many full-blood Cherokees, wore straight pins in their lapels to identify their opposition to the Echota pact.

Settling on virgin land with first pick of sites, Sallie and Robert Rogers Jr. had established a prosperous farm and business after moving from Big Tallapoosa, Georgia, to the Going Snake District that had been reserved for Cherokees under the 1835 treaty. In 1842, full-blood "pin" tribesmen who hated the treaty covertly crept upon the ranch and blacksmith operation and shot twenty-seven-year-old Robert Rogers Jr.

Killing Will's paternal grandfather undoubtedly was a mistake. After all, he was only twenty years old when the treaty was signed. The killing was one of three unsolved murders that impacted Will's life. The husband of Rogers' sister, May, was shot while preparing for bed and another male friend was slain while leaving May's frontier home.

Another gunplay incident marred Will Rogers' face. While he was a military academy cadet home for a visit, he grabbed a pal's rifle and began demonstrating the manual of arms. With the butt hitting the ground hard, the loaded rifle fired and the expended bullet left a graze mark up the left side of Will's face.

Betty and Will Rogers, a happily married couple. Will said he was a rarity in Hollywood because he kept the same wife he arrived with.

Years later, while a leading movie star, Will declined to play cinema cowboy roles such as those that glorified actors like Tom Mix, John Wayne and Roy Rogers (not his real name). In a silent-movie satire, he once depicted the stereotypical cowboy. Otherwise, he was unarmed. By birth, environment and training, Will was a genuine cowboy who showed little affection for pistols and was baffled by the need for automatics. He wrote that movies depicted guns as not having to be reloaded "no matter how many times a man may shoot a six-shooter in battle." Guns obviously had left more than a visual scar on the frontier man whose father had fought a bloody war.

VILLAINS ARE GETTING AS THICK AS COLLEGE DEGREES AND SOMETIMES ON THE SAME FELLOW.

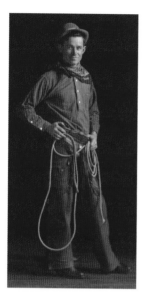

Publicity photos from the
Ziegfeld Follies days.

Except for brief excursions to two different boarding schools, the first ten years of Will's life were joyous with a happy family, a rich ranch and kindred pals. The scene changed May 28, 1890, when Mary fell ill and died of typhoid fever. Amid his grief, Clem presented ten-year-old Willie with Comanche, the first of many superb horses that Will owned throughout his life. Will was soon dispatched to a boarding school at Vinita, forty miles from the ranch, where he spent four years. He completed his ten years of formal education at Scarritt Collegiate Institute and Kemper Military Academy, both in Missouri.

In 1893, Clem, with his thirteen-year-old son riding in the caboose, shipped a train loaded with cattle to Chicago where a World's Fair gave the youngster his first glimpse of the world beyond the tall-grass prairie. World-famous Buffalo Bill was staging his Wild West Show with the "Congress of Rough Riders of the World" nearby. Young Will watched as gaudily attired Vicente Oropeza, billed as the greatest roper in the world, led a troupe of Mexican vaqueros. Horseback and afoot, Oropeza twirled a lariat

WHEN THE JUDGMENT DAY COMES, CIVILIZATION WILL HAVE AN ALIBI "I NEVER TOOK A HUMAN LIFE I ONLY SOLD THE FELLOW THE GUN TO TAKE IT WITH."

Will Rogers riding Teddy (named to honor President Theodore Roosevelt).

THEY WANT PEACE. BUT THEY WANT A GUN TO GET IT WITH.

that sketched the pattern for Will Rogers' career. With a flying rope, the Mexican wrote his name in the air, delighting the young lad. Will soon mastered all of Oropeza's rope tricks and invented new ones that he used later on stages around the world.

Late one night at age nineteen, Will simply walked away from the military academy and caught a train to west Texas. He became a $30-a-month cowboy and then a wrangler on cattle drives. His roping skills and horseman-ship were tested but his formal education had ended.

Back in Indian Territory, the U.S. government had mandated that Cherokee lands be divided into private allot-ments. Will, 9/32 Cherokee, was awarded seventy-nine acres of the family ranch that once spread across approxi-mately sixty thousand acres of grasslands.

Widowed Clem Rogers moved to the fledgling town of Claremore, where he became a business owner and banker as well as an elected delegate to write Oklahoma's constitution. At age twenty, Will meandered back to manage the ranching operations but was more interested in steer-roping contests and community dances.

The first publicity kit used by Will Rogers for lariat bookings.

Betty and Will Rogers shown with their three children, Will Jr., Mary, and Jim, sitting on his father's lap.

At the Oologah train station, a shy Will Rogers encountered Betty Blake, who was visiting her sister. During autumn evenings of 1899, Betty would play musical instruments and sing along with pals, including her "Injun cowboy" admirer. A romance was started, but then Betty went home to Rogers, Arkansas.

Over the next five years, Will and Betty corresponded irregularly. Restless and searching for adventure, Will sold his livestock and journeyed to Argentina, where he ran out of money and found little work. Landing a cattle-tending job on a slow freighter, he sailed to South Africa and won a part in Texas Jack's Wild West Show,

A MAN THAT DON'T LOVE A HORSE, THERE IS SOMETHING THE MATTER WITH HIM.

Will Rogers with son Will Jr. and daughter, Mary.

Sarah, a gentle calf, enjoyed free range in the Rogers family ranch home. Left to right are sons Will Jr. and Jim Rogers (hugging Sarah), wife Betty, daughter Mary and Will Rogers. This is in the front room of the home at the Will Rogers Historical Park, Pacific Palisades, California.

performing rope feats as a yelping American cowboy. Circumnavigating the Southern Hemisphere, Will performed in circuses in New Zealand and Australia before returning to the United States, where Wild West shows consumed his cowboy talents.

While playing Madison Square Garden, a rowdy steer broke loose, invaded the stands and terrified fans. Will calmly roped the animal and tugged him back to the arena. Newspapers heralded his heroism in the first of an onslaught of publicity that would skyrocket his career.

Will Rogers with a *Ziegfeld Follies* chorus line cast.

The 1928 Broadway musical comedy *Three Cheers* was scheduled to costar Fred Stone and his daughter, Dorothy. Fred was injured in a plane crash and Will Rogers stood in as the male lead. Shown left to right are Andy Toombes, Will Rogers, Dorothy Stone, Fred Stone (who was recovering) and Allene Stone, Fred's wife.

I MAINTAIN THAT IT SHOULD COST AS MUCH TO GET MARRIED AS IT DOES TO GET DIVORCED. MAKE IT LOOK LIKE MARRIAGE IS WORTH AS MUCH AS DIVORCE, EVEN IF IT AIN'T. THAT WOULD ALSO MAKE THE PREACHERS FINANCIALLY INDEPENDENT LIKE IT HAS THE LAWYERS.

"All I know is what I read in the papers" was a famous lead-off line in many of the four thousand newspaper columns in which Will Rogers' material appeared. He often read a half dozen or more newspapers each day.

"A Fellow of Infinite Jest"

While Will was playing at the 1904 World's Fair in St. Louis, Betty Blake caught his act, sent a note backstage and their romance was refueled with four more years of letter writing.

Vaudeville, at its peak of popularity, soon landed the talented roper, who fitted a horse with special shoes; he had a "sheriff" riding alongside while performing feats with his rope, looping both animal and man. They traveled coast to coast by train, earning a handsome $200 to $300 each week.

"Getting married," he wrote in his diary in November 1908 when he and Betty Blake, both 29, finally exchanged vows; then they caught a train to continue the show-business road tour. "The day I roped Betty," he wrote, "was the star performance of my life."

THERE AIN'T NOTHING TO LIFE BUT SATISFACTION.

Between moviemaking scenes, Will Rogers would retire to his automobile, retrieve his typewriter and peck out a daily newspaper column that was syndicated in several hundred newspapers.

In New York, he accidentally broke the silence of his act when the rope, on a miscue, snagged his cowboy boot: "Oops, I got all my legs through but one." The audience howled. Will was humiliated until the stage manager explained the laughter was a compliment. Assuming her first of many rewarding and major show-business management acts, Betty encouraged Will to continue talking on stage.

The change was explosive. In humble, down-home drawls Will Rogers began explaining his act, and then expanded into political commentary and jokes. "All I know is what I read in the papers" became his trademark. He kindly riveted Congress, joked about politicians and poked world leaders for their follies. He said the challenge was to "make jokes and tricks come out even. I have to either practice roping or learn more jokes."

Following years of concern about his son's wayward life in show business, Clem Rogers caught Will's vaudeville act in 1911 in Washington, D.C. He calculated the number of patrons and multiplied the ticket price. "Girls," he announced to his daughters, "that manager is sure making a lot of money off of Willie."

An early 1930s writer noted, "Scorning the art of make-up, with only a catch-as-catch-can knowledge of the intri-

Pilot Charles Lindbergh, the "Lone Eagle," and airplane passenger Will Rogers were photographed in 1927 alongside a Ford Tri-Motor aircraft. *Aviation Week* named both men among the top 100 figures in the history of aviation.

cate science of acting as known to Edwin Booth and Richard Mansfield and the Barrymores, he has become probably the most popular actor in this country."

With a decade as a performer, Will Rogers' main interest had become family. William Vann Rogers was born October 29, 1911, but was dubbed Will Rogers Jr. Days later at age seventy-two, Clem Vann Rogers died while asleep at his daughter's home in Chelsea, Oklahoma. His obituary writer said he was a "most philanthropic and public-spirited citizen . . . a friend of school children [who] amassed a fortune in his time but a large portion of it had been devoted to charity." Will Rogers also would earn a fortune and give large sums to good causes.

REMEMBER, WRITE TO YOUR CONGRESSMAN. EVEN IF HE CAN'T READ, WRITE TO HIM.

Will Rogers in a speech that
was broadcast by both NBC
and CBS.

In 1911, with an off-stage life and family business to
attend, Will purchased twenty prime acres in Claremore,
Oklahoma, as a home site. He began buying his sisters'
shares of the family ranch twelve miles north near
Oologah. While he visited family and friends at home
whenever possible, the dream house of Claremore never
was built because stage success and worldwide fame
kept him in the greater spotlight.

By 1917, Betty and Will Rogers had four children and still
contemplated leaving show business and becoming
Oklahoma ranchers. The rope-twirling cowboy comedian
was succeeding and prospering in various phases of
show business, including some Broadway musicals.

Then along came the incredible *Ziegfeld Follies*. While
beautiful actresses were the main draw, the show also
needed comedians. Flamboyant impresario Florenz

Ziegfeld recognized talent. Despite years on the stage, Will was quoted as saying: "Ziggy gave me my start." Between 1916 and 1925, Will Rogers headlined six of Ziegfeld's classical productions. Will explained that his job was to entertain the audience while the girls "changed from nothing into nothing." He read several newspapers daily, and the *Follies* was where Will began to extensively comment and joke about current events.

Will Rogers at a disaster-relief tent.

Will's observations, philosophical views and gentle criticism were noted and quoted by live audiences and reviewers, but Broadway attracted only a small portion of the American public. Book publishing magnified his messages greatly. In 1919, Harper & Brothers published *Rogers-isms: The Cowboy Philosopher on the Peace Conference.* He wrote that President Woodrow Wilson's World War I peace treaty "reads like a foreclosure." When Wilson appeared in the audience of one of his shows, Will continued his gentle barbs while the president roared with laughter.

The publishers followed with *Rogers-isms: The Cowboy Philosopher on Prohibition,* which ridiculed the anti-booze law but said that the "South is dry and will vote dry. That is, everybody that is sober enough to stagger to the polls will."

Will Rogers ad-libs during his regular network radio broadcast.

In 1922, the McNaught Syndicate recruited Will Rogers to write lengthy Sunday columns to subscribing newspapers led by the *New York Times*. These were touted as "humorous comment on contemporary affairs." Over the next thirteen years he wrote 666 columns of approximately a thousand words each. Often written weeks in advance, they were not timely, but many wondrous quotes and plainly spoken ideas were bundled within.

Then, from 1925 until 1935, Will Rogers wrote an additional 2,817 brief, poignant or funny daily columns. They were up-to-the-minute timely and terse. Newspapers splashed them prominently as "Will Rogers Says."

From time to time, up to six hundred newspapers with forty million readers paid to publish these works despite meshed grammar, misspelling and poor punctuation. He said when he "misspelled a few words, people said I was plain ignorant. But when I got all the words wrong, they declared I was a humorist."

"Please do not correct Will Rogers' English or spelling," a memo to editors at the *New York Times* admonished. "His little pieces are unique because he makes his own English. When you 'improve' it you are taking away part of the personality he is selling to readers."

I AM NO BELIEVER IN THIS "HARD WORK, PERSEVERANCE, AND TAKING ADVANTAGE OF YOUR OPPORTUNITIES" THAT THESE MAGAZINES ARE SO FOND OF WRITING SOME FELLOW UP IN. THE SUCCESSFUL DON'T WORK ANY HARDER THAN THE FAILURES. THEY GET WHAT IS CALLED IN BASEBALL THE BREAKS.

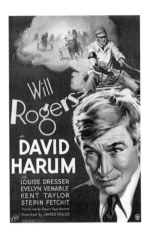

A 1934 *David Harum* movie poster. The movie starred Will Rogers as a shrewd banker and horse trader of upper New York State. "At the height of his form," wrote a *New York Times* reviewer of Rogers' performance. *Courtesy of Gordon Kuntz collection.*

WHY DON'T THEY PASS A CONSTITUTIONAL AMENDMENT PROHIBITING ANYBODY FROM LEARNING ANYTHING? IF IT WORKS AS GOOD AS PROHIBITION DID, IN FIVE YEARS WE WILL HAVE THE SMARTEST PEOPLE ON EARTH.

Even before he died in 1935, a small book said: "The true story of the rise of Will Rogers, the Cherokee Indian cowhand from Oologah, Indian Territory, is perhaps the most amazing tale that could be written about any living American . . . lacking the ability to turn out a paragraph that would pass the English teachers, he is one of America's highest-paid authors."

The older and more successful Will became, the writing got worse but the thinking got better. When asked if he read his own stuff, he said, "No, I get paid for writing, not reading." Newspaper column royalties reached $130,000 a year.

Will Rogers compiled the newspaper columns of 1923–24 to compose a book entitled *Illiterate Digest* that infuriated a lawyer for *Literary Digest,* but the author brushed off the criticism and calmed the critic through humor. Not every project succeeded. An attempt to create another newspaper column based on "The Worst Story I Heard Today" sputtered and failed.

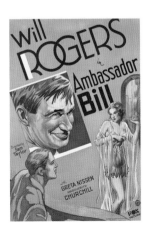

A 1931 *Ambassador Bill* movie poster. A *New York Times* reviewer wrote that the show "elicits plenty of chuckles." *Courtesy of Gordon Kuntz collection.*

Child star Shirley Temple posed with Will Rogers on the 20th Century Fox lot. Temple topped the 1935 box offices while Rogers slipped to number two after dominating the ratings in 1934 just ahead of Clark Gable.

Will Rogers starred as Hank in the 1931 Fox production of *A Connecticut Yankee,* which was based on the 1889 Mark Twain fantasy. Myrna Loy played the vamping Queen Morgan Le Fay. *Courtesy of Gordon Kuntz collection.*

Following a gall bladder operation, Will Rogers wrote *Ether and Me or "Just Relax,"* a hot seller. While critically ill, he still managed to file each of his daily newspaper columns and then recovered quickly to pen the book. Following his visit to Russia, he wrote *There's Not a Bathing Suit in Russia & Other Bare Facts,* claiming that while he didn't see all of the country, "I got to see all of some Russians," as men and women bathed together in a river. He also determined that vodka was Russia's national dissipation and advised "drink it down in a swig: nobody can sip vodka."

Covering a disarmament conference in Geneva in 1926, Will reported humorously for the *Saturday Evening Post* magazine, and then compiled his $2,000 articles into two books. Like his newspaper columns, the books were big moneymakers. How much? Decades after his father's death and his mother's demise nine years later, I asked his son Jim Rogers about Will Rogers' lifetime earnings.

"You'll never find out," he said. "When she was on her death bed, Mother told me that after I get all the business straightened out, for me to burn all the records. I did!"

Rare are financial trails at the expansive Will Rogers museum archives in Oklahoma. Equally scarce are copies of his actual signature.

Joe Levy of Evanston, Illinois, donated his massive Will Rogers collection in 1991 to the Claremore museum, adding original vaudeville contracts with weekly salaries of $300 and more along with rare Will Rogers signatures. There never was a contract with Flo Ziegfeld—Will Rogers said their hand-shake was sufficient. In Will's latter days, that friendship and deep trust led to Will paying for final doctor bills and for the 1932 burial of Ziegfeld, whose fortune had been lost in the financial crash of 1929.

The 1935 20th Century Fox talkie *Steamboat Round the Bend* starred Will Rogers as the quack doctor Jack Pearly, shown here with Francis Ford, the actor brother of John Ford, who was assistant director of the movie.

Beyond incredible earnings during the Depression, Will's greatest wealth came when income taxes were first launched and rates were low. He had actively purchased ranch land in Oklahoma and had expanded the family ranch in Santa Monica to more than four hundred acres, including a long stretch of beach abutting Pacific Palisades that he donated to the state of California for public use. When any luckless friend faced eviction, Will would assume ownership, make mortgage payments and allow the pal to keep a roof overhead, or he would simply hand out cash.

SOME PEOPLE SPEND A LIFETIME JUGGLING WITH WORDS, WITH NOT AN IDEA IN A CARLOAD.

Will Rogers, preparing to board a train on one of his many trips.

A wag of the mid-1930s said that during the final four years of his life, Will earned more than $1,500 a day. The estimate was conservative but would have totaled more than a half million per year in hard-time dollars. Earnings from early Wild West shows, vaudeville, the *Ziegfeld Follies,* magazine and newspaper columns, and books were dramatically paled by fees for sound-on-film movies. From 1918 to 1928, Will was well compensated for his fifty silent movies—$2,000 or $3,000 a week was common. Then he starred in twenty-one talkies that paid him more than $150,000 apiece. Fox, then 20th Century Fox Studio, earned more than $1 million on each feature.

The pay matched the pace. In those final sixty-six months of his life, Will Rogers averaged a new movie feature every ninety days, wrote 2,612 daily syndicated columns, filed 285 lengthy Sunday newspaper articles, circumnavigated the globe twice, encircled the South American continent by commercial plane, reported on two political conventions, played numerous polo matches, was a major radio commentator with a top Sunday night talk show, and delivered after-dinner speeches largely for charitable events. Still, he spent afternoons roping calves with his children and staging cookouts with family and pals.

THIS COUNTRY IS BIGGER THAN WALL STREET. IF THEY DON'T BELIEVE IT, I SHOW 'EM THE MAP.

More spectacular was his impact on the morale of
Americans during a dark period. Will Rogers' twenty-one
movies released during the early five years of the Great
Depression were wholesome, sometimes poignant, and
generally humorous, and they ended with an uplifting
moral. In fact, he veritably played himself regardless of
the role. Seldom would he learn a script but would speak
off-the-cuff for the cameras, enhancing the show. With
the exception of a sentence based on Mark Twain's
fantasy novel, he uttered this question to a knight in *A
Connecticut Yankee:* "Can you tell me where in the helleth
I am?" Otherwise, there was never profanity. For a dime,
patrons purchased an evening
of family entertainment
escaping Depression blues
without fearing "blue" cinema.

Will Rogers often weighed in
and paid postage for his weight
to fly aboard an early-day
airmail plane.

MARTINIQUE
ANTIGUA
GRENADA
TRINIDAD
COLOMBIA
COSTA RICA
NICARAGUA
BRIT. HONDURAS
DOMINICAN REPUBLIC
VIRGIN ISLANDS
St. LUCIA PORTO RICO
DOMINICA
VENEZUELA
PANAMA
CANAL ZONE   CUBA
HONDURAS   HAITI
MEXICO
GUAT
GUAL

Will Rogers prepares for takeoff as an open-cockpit airplane passenger.

Similar impact came on radios where he first started talking in 1922, complaining that it was "hard to make this little microphone laugh." Listeners laughed beyond his ear. His Sunday evening commentaries became so popular that churchgoers began skipping night services to hear him talk. Preachers were outraged. These were lighthearted gab sessions sometimes interfaced with tough talk about politics and economics. On one occasion after the market crash of 1929, his broadcast words, called the "Bacon, Beans and Limousine" speech, followed on-air remarks by President Herbert Hoover. Filmed for movie news reels, Will Rogers ad-libbed: "The only problem that confronts this country today is at least seven million people are out of work. . . . It's to see that every man that wants to, is able to work. Is allowed to find a place to go to work, and also to arrange some way of getting more equal distribution of wealth in the country. . . ."

In fact, by October 18, 1931, two years into a worldwide depression, men who had lost their fortunes were leaping from windows. Soup lines were common. Factories were closed. Fathers lost jobs. Hobos roamed the countryside, begging for food. Commerce was only a trickle. Will Rogers financed his own flying tour of the country, staging fund-raising shows, and he tossed his own money into the Red Cross' and Salvation Army's wars against hunger, poverty and despair. Amidst the Depression's sadness, people across the land gathered around radios to hear their poverty and plight articulated in Will Rogers' easily understood words. He offered cheer, hope and laughter.

Concluding the joint nationwide broadcast following the president, Will Rogers called on "every town and every city" to raise relief funds because "doggone it, people are liberal." He added, "They've got the money because there's as much money in the country as there ever was. Only fewer people have it." Finally, he had kind words for President Hoover's effort to reverse the economy, saying, "He's had a very tough uphill fight, and this will make him feel very good. He's a very human man."

Nonetheless, unemployment rose in the following year, the economy worsened and the government appeared

Traveling largely by steamship but by aircraft when possible, Will Rogers circumnavigated the globe three times. He is shown before an early-day American Airlines passenger plane.

Will Rogers in a movie-set still photo.

AMERICA CAN CARRY HERSELF AND GET ALONG IN PRETTY FAIR SHAPE, BUT WHEN SHE STOPS AND PICKS UP THE WHOLE WORLD AND PUTS IT ON HER SHOULDERS SHE JUST CAN'T "GET IT DONE."

powerless. With hope that the New Deal would spark recovery, Will endorsed and actively campaigned for Republican Hoover's opponent, Democrat Franklin D. Roosevelt, who won in a 1932 landslide.

Much credit for the victory went to Will Rogers. But, within a few months after radical changes were directed by Roosevelt, the pundit regained his nonpartisan stance. Will would pick and choose programs to oppose and support.

In 1928, before President Hoover was elected, Will had formally addressed both the Democratic and Republican national nominating conventions after *Life* magazine had cast him as a prank candidate. He swore that, if elected, his first action would be to resign. On one round of balloting, Will actually was nominated by Democrats. His quote "I'm not a member of any organized party—I'm a Democrat" dramatized the party's disarray that helped lead to Hoover's election.

"Look at the man," pundit H. L. Mencken of the *Baltimore Sun* fumed about Will Rogers and declared, "He alters foreign policies. He makes and unmakes candidates. He destroys public figures. By deriding Congress and undermining its prestige he has virtually reduced us to a monarchy. Millions of Americans read his words daily and those who are unable to read listen to him over the radio.

A FEW YEARS AGO WE WERE SO AFRAID THAT THE POOR PEOPLE WAS LIABLE TO TAKE A DRINK. NOW WE'VE FIXED IT SO THEY CAN'T EVEN GET SOMETHING TO EAT.

SO HERE WE ARE IN A COUNTRY WITH MORE WHEAT, MORE CORN AND MORE MONEY IN THE BANK, MORE COTTON, MORE EVERYTHING IN THE WORLD . . . AND YET WE'VE GOT PEOPLE STARVING. WE'LL HOLD THE DISTINCTION OF BEING THE ONLY NATION IN THE HISTORY OF THE WORLD THAT EVER WENT TO THE POOR HOUSE IN AN AUTOMOBILE.

. . . THE MOST UNEMPLOYED OR THE HUNGRIEST MAN IN AMERICA HAS CONTRIBUTED IN SOME WAY TO THE WEALTH OF EVERY MILLIONAIRE IN AMERICA. IT WAS THE BIG BOYS THEMSELVES WHO THOUGHT THIS FINAN-CIAL DRUNK WE WERE GOING THROUGH WAS GOING TO LAST FOREVER. THEY OVER-MERGED AND OVER-CAPITALIZED AND OVER-EVERYTHING ELSE. THAT'S THE FIX WE'RE IN NOW.

I consider him the most dangerous writer alive today." "Come on now, Henry," Will replied. "You know that nobody with any sense ever took any of my gags seriously."

Mencken shot back: "They are taken seriously by nobody except half-wits, in other words by approximately 85 percent of the voting population."

Suggestions that Will Rogers should stick to comedy and draw back from political commentary triggered a reply in his column: "I have written on nothing but poli-tics for years. You never hear me on a mother-in-law joke. It is always about national or international affairs."

THE DIFFERENCE BETWEEN OUR RICH AND POOR GROWS GREATER EVERY YEAR. OUR DISTRIBUTION OF WEALTH IS GETTING MORE UNEVEN ALL THE TIME. A MAN CAN MAKE A MILLION AND HE IS ON EVERY PAGE IN THE MORNING. BUT IT NEVER TELLS YOU WHO GAVE UP THAT MILLION HE GOT. YOU CAN'T GET MONEY WITHOUT TAKING IT FROM SOMEBODY.

Extensive travel, reading many newspapers and, as he said, "associating with smarter people" provided his sources. He meandered across war-torn China, reporting on the Japanese invasion, and he took a seven-day train ride from the east to the west of the Soviet Union in his second visit to the Communist nation. He traveled all over Europe and visited Latin American countries as well.

Gaining audiences with most of the world leaders whom he sought to meet, Will developed views and wrote boldly. While the winds of World War II were beginning to swell, Will spent an hour with Italian dictator Mussolini, failed to gain an interview with Germany's Hitler and sipped tea with Japan's war minister. His reviews were mixed, sometimes even inconsistent. Like the average American whom he personified, Will switched views from time to time.

Will warned that America could not find "a better fight to stay out of" than Japan's escalating war with China. Recognizing financial investments by Japan in Manchuria, he sized up the war with an analogy: "China owns the lot, Japan owns the house that's on it, now who is going to furnish the policeman?"

WHEN NEWSPAPERS KNOCK A MAN A LOT, THERE IS SURE TO BE A LOT OF GOOD IN HIM.

A few weeks before his death, Will got a preview of Boeing's prototype B-17, the "flying fortress." "If we don't

While he never was a pilot, Will Rogers loved aircraft and never was shy about posing for a photo to champion aviation.

want it Abyssinia does," he quipped about the bomber six years before the attack on Pearl Harbor. The United States bought the bomber to obliterate Japan.

Aviation was a love affair that started in 1915 when Will took his first flight at Atlantic City. Commercially, in charter flights and even paying per-pound postage to ride in airmail planes, Will increasingly utilized and championed aviation. He also survived plane crashes but downplayed the dangers. In 1925, General Billy Mitchell flew Will over Washington, D.C., and recruited the influential writer to his controversial battle for a U.S. air force. Mitchell was court-martialed and drummed out of the service for his outspokenness while some eight decades later, at the Paris Air Show, Will was proclaimed a top force in the history of aviation for his outspokenness.

Aviator Wiley Post was a one-eyed fellow Oklahoman who flew around the world twice—once solo in a plywood plane with one engine. Will was enchanted, wrote glowingly

WE ELECT OUR PRESIDENTS, BE THEY REPUBLICAN OR DEMOCRAT, THEN START DARING 'EM TO MAKE GOOD.

One-eyed aviator Wiley Post and Will Rogers, 1935.

about Post and struck up a friendship with him. In a new single-engine plane, the pair decided to explore Alaska, making the first transpolar flight from Point Barrow to Moscow.

After zigzagging across the territory and parts of Canada, they took off August 15, 1935, from Fairbanks en route to the northernmost point of the American continent. The sky was overcast as they droned north-ward with virtually no guidance, as magnetic compasses lose their value so close to the pole. Eight hours aloft, Post spotted a break in the cloud cover, dipped low and spied an Eskimo hunting camp on an inlet of the Arctic Ocean. The pontoons worked perfectly for a landing. Startled, the hunters pointed toward Point Barrow a dozen miles northward.

IT TAKES NERVE TO BE A DEMOCRAT, BUT
IT TAKES MONEY TO BE A REPUBLICAN.

Post, thirty-five and wearing his trademark eye patch, returned to the cockpit and Will Rogers, fifty-five, lodged himself in the extreme rear of the plane for balance. A typewriter at his side held the text of a newspaper column that recanted a yarn about a fox terrier's run-in with a bear that had to be shot. The last word typed was "death."

Eskimos estimated that the plane roared to an altitude of fifty to two hundred feet when it curled in the air and plunged into four feet of water. There was no fire. The Eskimos called out "Halloo! Halloo!" Silence. An elder began a historic fifteen-mile run to Point Barrow, reporting, "Red bird crashed. Two men. One with sick eye." Boats were launched and sped toward the scene. Will Rogers' body had been recovered and laid in a sleeping bag from the plane. Post was impaled by the engine and the wreckage was torn apart to collect his remains. The cause of the crash never was ascertained. Perhaps they ran out of gasoline or a sliver of ice plugged the carburetor.

An army sergeant telegraphed the news. Saturday newspapers around the world headlined the story. The

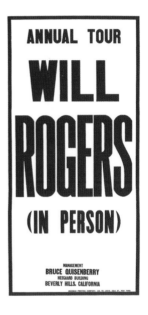

ANNUAL TOUR

WILL ROGERS

(IN PERSON)

MANAGEMENT
BRUCE QUISENBERRY
HEEGAARD BUILDING
BEVERLY HILLS, CALIFORNIA

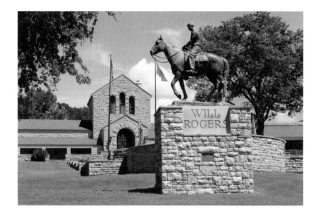

The Will Rogers Memorial Museum in Claremore, Oklahoma, with Will Rogers on Soapsuds. Sculpted by Electra Waggoner, the statue was named *Riding into the Sunset.* Will Rogers and members of the family are reposed in a tomb behind the statue.

Will Rogers' two sons, Will Jr. and Jim, remained active in keeping their father's legacy alive until their own deaths. Will Jr. starred in *The Story of Will Rogers,* and Jim, shown with the cowboy hat, was a lifetime cattleman.

networks went silent in reverence. Planes towing black banners flew over New York. Folks wept on the streets. More than fifty thousand people walked past the bier of Will Rogers, and the Hollywood Bowl staged his public funeral following private family ceremonies. Post's body was delivered to the Oklahoma capital and he was buried nearby.

Temporarily interred in California, Will Rogers' body was moved eight years later to a handsome tomb on the twenty acres where he had planned a retirement home. Instead, it now hosted the publicly funded Will Rogers Memorial Museum.

Betty Rogers donated the Claremore land to the state of Oklahoma for a free nine-gallery museum named the Will Rogers Memorial Museum. Using four hundred acres of the original property, the ranch remained open daily to the public as the 1879 living-history birthplace ranch of Will Rogers, complete with longhorn cattle and other farm animals, with the log-walled house presiding.

A life-size oil-on-canvas portrayal of Will Rogers by Charles Banks Wilson. This painting greets visitors at the Claremore museum. Joe Carter, author of this book, commissioned the portrait and, as a model, donned the suit that Will Rogers wore the day of the fatal crash. Jim Rogers, Will's son, was Wilson's model for the facial colors.

SOMEBODY IS ALWAYS TELLING US IN THE PAPERS HOW TO PREVENT WAR. THERE IS ONLY ONE WAY IN THE WORLD TO PREVENT WAR, AND THAT IS, FOR EVERY NATION TO TEND TO ITS OWN BUSINESS.

Five years before Will's death, in a pulpit in Boston, he said: "When I die my epitaph or whatever you call those signs on gravestones is going to read 'I joked about every prominent man of my time but I never met a man I didn't like.' I am so proud of that I can hardly wait to die so it can be carved. And when you come around my grave you'll probably find me sitting there proudly reading it."

And so the words remain carved in granite.

LIVE YOUR LIFE SO THAT WHENEVER YOU LOSE, YOU ARE AHEAD.

GOVERNMENT & POLITICS

THE REPUBLICAN PLATFORM PROMISES TO DO BETTER. I DON'T THINK THEY HAVE DONE SO BAD. EVERYBODY'S BROKE BUT THEM.

★

DEMOCRATS TAKE THE WHOLE THING AS A JOKE. REPUBLICANS TAKE IT SERIOUS BUT RUN IT LIKE A JOKE.

★

I WILL ADMIT IT HAS RAINED MORE UNDER REPUBLICAN ADMINISTRATIONS. THAT WAS PARTIALLY BECAUSE THEY HAVE HAD MORE ADMINISTRATION THAN DEMOCRATS.

★

THE PLATFORM WILL ALWAYS BE THE SAME, PROMISE EVERYTHING, DELIVER NOTHING.

★

A CANNIBAL IS A GOOD DEAL LIKE A DEMOCRAT, THEY ARE FORCED TO LIVE OFF EACH OTHER.

★

REPUBLICANS TAKE CARE OF BIG MONEY, FOR BIG MONEY TAKES CARE OF THEM.

★

I HAVE NOT ALIGNED MYSELF WITH ANY PARTY. SITTING TIGHT WAITING FOR AN ATTRACTIVE OFFER.

★

I GENERALLY GIVE THE PARTY IN POWER, WHETHER REPUBLICAN OR DEMOCRAT, THE MORE DIGS BECAUSE THEY ARE GENERALLY DOING THE COUNTRY MORE DAMAGE. THE PARTY IN POWER DRAWING A SALARY IS TO BE KNOCKED.

★

I HOPE SOME OF THE MEN WHO GET THE MOST VOTES WILL BE ELECTED.

★

Will Rogers with Vice President John Nance Garner, former Speaker of the U.S. House of Representatives.

A FLOCK OF DEMOCRATS WILL REPLACE A MESS OF REPUBLICANS. . . . IT WON'T MEAN A THING. THEY WILL GO IN LIKE ALL THE REST OF 'EM. GO IN ON PROMISES AND COME OUT ON ALIBIS.

THE REPUBLICANS MOPPED UP, THE DEMOCRATS GUMMED UP, AND I WILL NOW TRY AND SUM UP. THINGS ARE TERRIBLY DULL NOW. WE WON'T HAVE ANY MORE SERIOUS COMEDY UNTIL CONGRESS MEETS.

YOU'VE GOT TO ADMIT THAT EACH PARTY IS WORSE THAN THE OTHER. THE ONE THAT'S OUT ALWAYS LOOKS THE BEST.

IF A MAN WANTS TO STAND WELL SOCIALLY, HE CAN'T AFFORD TO BE SEEN WITH EITHER THE DEMOCRATS OR THE REPUBLICANS.

REPUBLICANS WANT A MAN THAT CAN LEND DIGNITY TO THE OFFICE. DEMOCRATS WANT A MAN THAT WILL LEND SOME MONEY.

REPUBLICANS HAVE ALWAYS BEEN THE PARTY OF BIG BUSINESS. THE DEMOCRATS OF SMALL BUSINESS. SO YOU JUST TAKE YOUR PICK. THE DEMOCRATS HAVE THEIR EYE ON A DIME AND THE REPUBLICANS ON A DOLLAR.

IF BY SOME DIVINE ACT OF PROVIDENCE WE COULD GET RID OF BOTH PARTIES AND HIRE SOME GOOD MEN, LIKE ANY OTHER GOOD BUSINESS DOES, THAT WOULD BE SITTING PRETTY.

Will Rogers and Eleanor
Roosevelt, the nation's
first lady.

BOTH PARTIES HAVE THEIR GOOD TIMES AND BAD TIMES AT DIFFERENT TIMES. GOOD WHEN THEY ARE OUT. BAD WHEN THEY ARE IN.

★

THERE AIN'T ANY FINER FOLKS LIVING THAN A REPUBLICAN THAT VOTES THE DEMOCRATIC TICKET.

★

OHIO CLAIMS THEY ARE DUE A PRESIDENT AS THEY HAVEN'T HAD ONE SINCE TAFT. LOOK AT THE UNITED STATES, THEY HAVE NOT HAD ONE SINCE LINCOLN.

★

YOU COULD KEEP POLITICS CLEAN IF YOU COULD FIGURE OUT SOME WAY SO YOUR GOVERNMENT NEVER HIRED ANYONE.

★

NO MATHEMATICIAN IN THIS COUNTRY HAS EVER BEEN ABLE TO FIGURE OUT HOW MANY HUNDRED STRAW VOTES IT TAKES TO EQUAL ONE LEGITIMATE VOTE.

★

NO ANIMAL IN THE WORLD GETS QUITE AS HUNGRY AS A DEMOCRAT. HE WOULD RATHER MAKE A SPEECH THAN A DOLLAR.

★

THE WHOLE TROUBLE WITH THE REPUBLICANS IS THEIR FEAR OF AN INCREASE IN INCOME TAX, ESPECIALLY ON HIGHER INCOMES.

★

SOMETIMES IT MAKES YOU THINK WE DON'T NEED A DIFFERENT MAN AS MUCH AS WE NEED DIFFERENT ADVISORS FOR THE SAME MAN.

★

At the Hollywood Bowl in 1932, Will Rogers humorously introduced presidential hopeful Franklin D. Roosevelt, who reared back in laughter. Roosevelt's son is at the candidate's side.

IF WE COULD JUST SEND THE SAME BUNCH OF MEN TO WASHINGTON FOR THE GOOD OF THE NATION AND NOT FOR POLITICAL REASONS, WE COULD HAVE THE MOST PERFECT GOVERNMENT IN THE WORLD.

THE TRUTH CAN HURT YOU WORSE IN AN ELECTION THAN ABOUT ANYTHING THAT COULD HAPPEN TO YOU.

MORE MEN HAVE BEEN ELECTED BETWEEN SUNDOWN AND SUNUP, THAN EVER WERE ELECTED BETWEEN SUNUP AND SUNDOWN.

POLITICS AIN'T WORRYING THIS COUNTRY ONE TENTH AS MUCH AS PARKING SPACE.

A POLITICIAN IS JUST LIKE A PICKPOCKET. IT'S ALMOST IMPOSSIBLE TO GET ONE TO REFORM.

PARTY POLITICS IS THE MOST NARROW MINDED OCCUPATION IN THE WORLD.

IF YOU EVER INJECTED TRUTH INTO POLITICS YOU HAVE NO POLITICS.

AIN'T IT FUNNY HOW MANY HUNDREDS OF THOUSANDS OF SOLDIERS WE CAN RECRUIT WITH NERVE. BUT WE CAN'T FIND ONE POLITICIAN IN A MILLION WITH BACKBONE.

Will Rogers with John D.
Rockefeller and two ladies.

MOST PEOPLE AND ACTORS APPEARING ON THE STAGE HAVE SOME WRITER TO WRITE THEIR MATERIAL. CONGRESS IS GOOD ENOUGH FOR ME. THEY HAVE BEEN WRITING MY MATERIAL FOR YEARS.

★

ALL SENATORS TRAVEL A LOT. THEY ALL TRY TO KEEP AWAY FROM HOME AS MUCH AS THEY CAN.

★

WHY SLEEP AT HOME WHEN YOU CAN SLEEP IN CONGRESS?

★

BE A POLITICIAN—NO TRAINING NECESSARY.

★

IT IS EASIER TO FOOL 'EM IN WASHINGTON THAN AT HOME. SO WHY NOT BE A SENATOR.

★

GET IN THE CABINET; YOU WON'T HAVE TO STAY LONG.

★

BE A REPUBLICAN AND SOONER OR LATER YOU WILL BE A POSTMASTER.

★

YOU KNOW HOW CONGRESS IS. THEY'LL VOTE FOR ANYTHING IF THE THING THEY VOTE FOR WILL TURN AROUND AND VOTE FOR THEM.

★

PAPERS SAY: "CONGRESS IS DEADLOCKED AND CAN'T ACT." I THINK THAT IS THE GREATEST BLESSING THAT COULD BEFALL THIS COUNTRY.

★

ONE SELDOM EVER REMEMBERS MEETING A VICE-PRESIDENT.

★

I JOKE ABOUT PROMINENT MEN BUT AT HEART I BELIEVE IN 'EM. I DO THINK
THERE IS TIME WHEN TRACES OF "DUMBNESS" CROP UP IN OFFICIAL LIFE
BUT NOT CROOKEDNESS.

★

ELECTIONS ARE A GOOD DEAL LIKE MARRIAGES. THERE'S NO ACCOUNTING
FOR ANYONE'S TASTE.

★

IT'S AWFUL HARD TO GET PEOPLE INTERESTED IN CORRUPTION UNLESS THEY
CAN GET SOME OF IT.

★

IT'S GOING TO BE HARD TO MAKE AN ISSUE OF CORRUPTION. IT'S LIKE THE POOR,
IT'S ALWAYS BEEN WITH US.

★

WE CUSS THE LAWMAKERS. BUT I NOTICE WE'RE ALWAYS PERFECTLY WILLING TO
SHARE IN ANY OF THE SUMS OF MONEY THAT THEY MIGHT DISTRIBUTE.

★

EVERYBODY NOWADAYS IS SUGGESTING WAYS OF GETTING PROSPEROUS ON
SOMEBODY ELSE'S MONEY.

★

BEING SERIOUS OR BEING A GOOD FELLOW HAS GOT NOTHING TO DO WITH RUNNING
THIS COUNTRY. IF THE BREAKS ARE WITH YOU, YOU COULD BE A LAUGHING HYENA
AND STILL HAVE A GREAT ADMINISTRATION.

★

THERE IS PEOPLE SO EXCITED OVER THIS ELECTION THAT THEY THINK THE PRESIDENT
HAS SOMETHING TO DO WITH RUNNING THIS COUNTRY.

★

The late Kansas City artist Frank Szasz used a set still from *Judge Priest* for this painting of Will Rogers. Szasz painted the eyes brown while all records indicate and his family verified that Will Rogers' eyes were blue.

IF I WAS A PRESIDENT AND WANTED SOMETHING I WOULD CLAIM I DIDN'T WANT IT. CONGRESS HAS NOT GIVEN ANY PRESIDENT ANYTHING HE WANTED IN THE LAST 10 YEARS. BE AGAINST ANYTHING AND THEN HE IS SURE TO GET IT.

POLITICS IS THE ONLY SPORTING EVENT IN THE WORLD WHERE THEY DON'T PAY OFF FOR SECOND MONEY; A MAN TO RUN SECOND IN ANY OTHER EVENT IN THE WORLD IT'S AN HONOR. BUT ANY TIME HE RUNS SECOND FOR PRESIDENT IT'S NOT AN HONOR. IT'S A PITY.

A PRESIDENT SHOULD HOLD OFFICE SIX YEARS WITH NO RE-ELECTION. STOP THIS THING OF A PRESIDENT HAVING TO LOWER HIS DIGNITY AND GO TROOPING AROUND ASKING FOR VOTES TO KEEP HIM ANOTHER TERM. SIX YEARS GIVE HIM TIME TO DO SOMETHING. THEN PAY THE MAN WHEN HE GOES OUT ONE-HALF OF HIS SALARY FOR LIFE.

GEORGE WASHINGTON WAS A POLITICIAN AND A GENTLEMAN. THAT'S A RARE COMBINATION.

LINCOLN DIDN'T HAVE A FOREIGN POLICY. THAT'S WHY HE'S LINCOLN.

THEY OUGHT TO PASS A RULE IN THIS COUNTRY IN ANY INVESTIGATIONS, IF A MAN COULDN'T TELL THE TRUTH THE FIRST TIME HE SHOULDN'T BE ALLOWED TO TRY AGAIN.

★

Mickey Rooney was a child player in the 1935 movie *The County Chairman,* starring Will Rogers. Six decades later, Rooney played Will Rogers' father, Clem, in the Broadway musical *The Will Rogers Follies: A Life in Revue.*

JUST RAID THE NATIONAL TREASURY ENOUGH AND YOU WILL SOON BE REFERRED TO AS A "STATESMAN."

★

STATISTICS HAVE PROVEN THAT THE SUREST WAY TO GET ANYTHING OUT OF THE PUBLIC MIND AND NEVER HEAR OF IT AGAIN IS TO HAVE A SENATE COMMITTEE APPOINTED TO LOOK INTO IT.

★

YOU WIRE THE STATE OR THE FEDERAL GOVERNMENT THAT OUR COW OR HOG IS SICK AND THEY WILL SEND OUT EXPERTS FROM WASHINGTON AND APPROPRIATE MONEY TO ERADICATE THE CAUSE. YOU WIRE THEM THAT YOUR BABY HAS THE DIPHTHERIA OR SCARLET FEVER AND SEE WHAT THEY DO. . . . WHY CAN'T WE GET A GOVERNMENT TO AT LEAST DO FOR A CHILD'S PROTECTION, WHAT THEY DO FOR A COW OR A HOG?

★

AFTER A FOOTBALL GAME IN LIMA, PERU, FIVE WERE KILLED. UP HERE WE DON'T KILL OUR FOOTBALL PLAYERS. WE MAKE COACHES OUT OF THE SMART ONES AND SEND THE OTHERS TO THE LEGISLATURE.

★

THE AMERICAN PEOPLE WILL VOTE DRY AS LONG AS THEY ARE ABLE TO STAGGER TO THE POLLS.

★

THE MORE EDUCATION HE GETS THE LESS APT HE IS TO BE A DEMOCRAT, AND IF HE IS VERY HIGHLY EDUCATED HE WILL SEE THE APPLE SAUCE IN BOTH PARTIES.

★

CONFUCIUS PERSPIRED OUT MORE KNOWLEDGE THAN THE U.S. SENATE HAS VOCALIZED OUT IN THE LAST 50 YEARS.

★

FARMERS ARE LEARNING THE RELIEF THEY GET FROM THE SKY BEATS WHAT THEY GET FROM WASHINGTON.

★

NONE OF THEM FROM ANY PARTY ARE GOING TO PURPOSELY RUIN THE COUNTRY. THEY WILL ALL DO THE BEST THEY CAN.

★

THIS COUNTRY HAS GOTTEN WHERE IT IS IN SPITE OF POLITICS, NOT BY THE AID OF IT.

★

PEOPLE DON'T CHANGE UNDER GOVERNMENTS. GOVERNMENTS CHANGE. PEOPLE REMAIN THE SAME.

★

ONE OF THE EVILS OF DEMOCRACY IS YOU HAVE TO PUT UP WITH THE MAN YOU ELECTED WHETHER YOU WANT HIM OR NOT. THAT'S WHY WE CALL IT DEMOCRACY.

★

EVERY GUY LOOKS IN HIS POCKET AND THEN VOTES.

★

THE SHORT MEMORIES OF AMERICAN VOTERS IS WHAT KEEPS OUR POLITICIANS IN OFFICE.

★

ONCE A MAN HOLDS PUBLIC OFFICE, HE IS ABSOLUTELY NO GOOD FOR HONEST WORK.

★

AS BAD AS WE SOMETIMES THINK OUR GOVERNMENT IS RUN, IT IS THE BEST RUN I EVER SAW.

★

Will Rogers with friends alongside an airplane.

THE HIGH OFFICE OF PRESIDENT HAS BEEN DEGENERATED INTO TWO ORDINARILY FINE MEN BEING GOADED ON BY POLITICAL LEECHES INTO SAYING THINGS THAT IF THEY WERE IN THEIR RIGHT MINDS THEY WOULDN'T THINK OF SAYING.

★

IN THIS COUNTRY PEOPLE DON'T VOTE FOR, THEY VOTE AGAINST.

★

A STATESMAN IS A MAN THAT CAN DO WHAT THE POLITICIAN WOULD LIKE TO DO BUT CAN'T BECAUSE HE IS AFRAID OF NOT BEING ELECTED.

★

THERE IS VERY LITTLE DIGNITY, VERY LITTLE SPORTSMANSHIP, OR VERY LITTLE ANYTHING IN POLITICS ONLY GET THE JOB AND HOLD IT.

★

WHEN AN OFFICE HOLDER, OR ONE THAT HAS BEEN FOUND OUT, CAN'T THINK OF ANYTHING TO DELIVER A SPEECH ON, HE ALWAYS FALLS BACK ON THE GOOD OLD SUBJECT, AMERICANISM.

★

NOTHING WILL UPSET A STATE ECONOMIC CONDITION LIKE A LEGISLATURE. IT'S BETTER TO HAVE TERMITES IN YOUR HOUSE THAN THE LEGISLATURE.

★

THE MONEY WE SPEND ON GOVERNMENT. AND IT'S NOT A BIT BETTER GOVERNMENT THAN WE GOT FOR ONE-THIRDS THE MONEY TWO YEARS AGO.

★

NEVER BLAME A LEGISLATIVE BODY FOR NOT DOING SOMETHING. WHEN THEY DO NOTHING, THEY DON'T HURT ANYBODY. IT'S WHEN THEY DO SOMETHING IS WHEN THEY GET DANGEROUS.

★

Will Rogers with Broadway song and dance star Fred Stone and artist Ed Borein at the Fiesta celebration in Santa Barbara, California, circa 1929.

A SMART STATE NOWADAYS WILL APPOINT ALL THEIR HIGHWAY MEN FROM ONE PLACE. THEN ONE ROAD WILL DO ALL OF 'EM.

★

ALL THERE IS TO POLITICS IS TRADING. THAT'S WHY POLITICS IS NOT AS GOOD AS IT WAS YEARS AGO. THEY DON'T HAVE AS MANY OLD-TIME HORSE TRADERS IN THERE. THESE WE GOT ARE JUST AMATEURS. THEY'RE CRUDE WITH THEIR TRADES. THERE IS REALLY NO "FINESSE." YOU MIGHT NOT GET THAT. "FINESSE" IS A FRENCH WORD AND IT MEANS SNEAKING IT OVER.

★

WHAT THIS COUNTRY NEEDS IS MORE WORKING MEN AND FEWER POLITICIANS.

★

THAT'S THE TROUBLE WITH A POLITICIAN'S LIFE SOMEBODY IS ALWAYS INTER-RUPTING IT WITH AN ELECTION.

★

IMAGINE A MAN IN PUBLIC OFFICE THAT EVERYBODY KNEW WHERE HE STOOD. WE WOULDN'T CALL HIM A STATESMAN, WE WOULD CALL HIM A CURIOSITY.

★

THERE SHOULD BE A TAX ON EVERY MAN THAT WANTED TO GET A GOVERNMENT APPOINTMENT OR BE ELECTED TO OFFICE. IN TWO YEARS THAT TAX ALONE WOULD PAY OUR NATIONAL DEBT.

★

THE UNITED STATES SENATE OPENS WITH A PRAYER AND CLOSES WITH AN INVESTIGATION.

★

Spencer Tracy with Will Rogers
imitating Spencer Tracy.

THE WAYS AND MEANS COMMITTEE IS SUPPOSED TO
FIND WAYS TO DIVIDE UP
THE MEANS.

★

A CONSERVATIVE IS A MAN WHO HAS PLENTY OF MONEY AND DOESN'T SEE ANY
REASON WHY HE SHOULD ALWAYS HAVE PLENTY OF MONEY. A DEMOCRAT IS A
FELLOW WHO NEVER HAD ANY MONEY BUT DOESN'T SEE WHY HE SHOULDN'T.

★

THERE IS NO MORE INDEPENDENCE IN POLITICS THAN THERE IS IN JAIL. THEY ARE
ALWAYS YAPPING ABOUT "PUBLIC SERVICE." IT'S PUBLIC JOBS THAT THEY ARE
LOOKING FOR.

★

I LOVE ANIMALS AND I LOVE POLITICIANS. I LIKE TO WATCH BOTH OF 'EM PLAY,
EITHER BACK HOME IN THEIR NATIVE STATE OR AFTER THEY HAVE BEEN CAPTURED
AND SENT TO A ZOO OR TO WASHINGTON.

★

A LOBBYIST IS A PERSON THAT IS SUPPOSED TO HELP A POLITICIAN MAKE UP HIS
MIND—NOT ONLY HELP HIM BUT PAY HIM.

★

THE BIGGEST PRAISE THAT A HUMORIST CAN HAVE IS TO GET YOUR STUFF IN *THE
CONGRESSIONAL RECORD*. JUST THINK, MY NAME WILL BE RIGHT ALONGSIDE ALL
THOSE OTHER BIG HUMORISTS.

★

THERE IS NO RACE OF PEOPLE IN THE WORLD THAT CAN COMPETE WITH A SENATOR
FOR TALKING. IF I WENT TO THE SENATE, I COULDN'T TALK FAST ENOUGH TO
ANSWER ROLL CALL.

★

Will Rogers in mukluk boots in Alaska during the final days of his life, 1935.

ABOUT BEING A U.S. SENATOR, THE ONLY THING THE LAW SAYS YOU HAVE TO BE IS 30 YEARS OLD. NOT ANOTHER SINGLE REQUIREMENT. THEY JUST FIGURE THAT A MAN THAT OLD GOT NOBODY TO BLAME BUT HIMSELF IF HE GETS CAUGHT THERE.

★

I LIKE TO MAKE JOKES AND KID ABOUT THE SENATORS. THEY ARE A NEVER-ENDING SOURCE OF AMUSEMENT, AMAZEMENT AND DISCOURAGEMENT. BUT THE RASCALS, WHEN YOU MEET 'EM THEY ARE MIGHTY NICE FELLOWS. IT MUST BE SOMETHING IN THE OFFICE THAT MAKES THEM SO ORNERY SOMETIMES. WHEN YOU SEE WHAT THEY DO OFFICIAL, YOU WANT TO SHOOT 'EM. BUT WHEN HE LOOKS AT YOU AND GRINS SO INNOCENTLY, YOU KINDER WANT TO KISS HIM.

IT WON'T BE NO TIME UNTIL SOME WOMAN WILL BECOME SO DESPERATE POLITI-CALLY AND LOSE ALL PROSPECTUS OF RIGHT AND WRONG AND MAYBE GO FROM BAD TO WORSE AND FINALLY WIND UP IN THE SENATE. MEN GAVE 'EM THE RIGHT TO VOTE BUT NEVER MEANT FOR THEM TO TAKE IT SERIOUSLY. BUT BEING WOMEN THEY TOOK THE WRONG MEANING AND DID.

★

IT MUST BE NICE TO BELONG TO SOME LEGISLATIVE BODY AND JUST PICK MONEY OUT OF THE AIR.

★

DEMOCRATS, YOU CAN'T SHAME THEM INTO EVEN DYING. THEY WOULD KEEP ON LIVING JUST TO SPITE THE REPUBLICANS.

Will Rogers simultaneously ropes "Sheriff" Buck McKee and his horse, Teddy, in their vaudeville act.

OUTSIDE OF TRAFFIC, THERE IS NOTHING THAT HAS HELD THIS COUNTRY BACK AS MUCH AS COMMITTEES.

EVERYBODY IN WASHINGTON SEEMS TO BE APOLOGIZING TO EACH OTHER. IN WASHINGTON THEY JUST GENERALLY FIGURE THAT ONE HATRED OFFSETS THE OTHER AND THEY ARE BOTH EVEN.

THESE BACCALAUREATE ADDRESSES GIVEN TO GRADUATES DON'T OFFER 'EM MUCH ENCOURAGEMENT OUTSIDE OF ADVISING 'EM TO VOTE THE STRAIGHT REPUBLICAN TICKET.

THIS COUNTRY JUST CIVIC LUNCHEONED ITSELF INTO DEPRESSION. IF THEY WILL ALL GO HOME AND EAT WITH THEIR OWN FAMILIES, THEY WILL NOT ONLY GET THEIR FIRST GOOD LUNCH IN YEARS, BUT WILL BE SURPRISED HOW MUCH MORE INTELLIGENTLY THEIR OWN WIFE CAN TALK THAN THE "SPEAKER OF THE DAY."

I HAVE LOOKED POLITICS AND THE MOVIES BOTH OVER AND, WHILE THEY HAVE MUCH IN COMMON I BELIEVE POLITICS IS THE MOST COMMON, SO I WILL STAY WITH THE MOVIES.

TAX RELIEF, FARM RELIEF, FLOOD RELIEF, DAM RELIEF—NONE OF THESE HAVE BEEN SETTLED, BUT THEY ARE GETTING THEM IN SHAPE FOR CONSIDERATION AT THE NEXT SESSION OF CONGRESS WITH THE HOPE THAT THOSE NEEDING RELIEF WILL PERHAPS HAVE CONVENIENTLY DIED IN THE MEANTIME.

John Ford was assistant director under Sol Wurtzel in the 1935 20th Century Fox film *Steamboat Round the Bend*. Irvin S. Cobb, who wrote the novel, played a rival steamboat captain in the movie starring Will Rogers. The picture was released four days following the fatal crash in Alaska that claimed the lives of Wiley Post and Will Rogers, which left the world in mourning. Patron reaction was twisted by the reality of the death while the movie was described as a "fast, laughter-laden farce" by a reviewer. *Courtesy of Gordon Kuntz collection.*

I HAVE READ ALL PRESIDENTIAL SPEECHES ON BOTH SIDES UP TO NOW, AND THE WINNER IS THE MAN SMART ENOUGH TO NOT MAKE ANY MORE. THERE IS A GREAT CHANCE FOR A "SILENT" THIRD PARTY.

★

A PRESIDENT-ELECT'S POPULARITY IS THE SHORTEST LIVED OF ANY PUBLIC MAN. IT ONLY LASTS TILL HE PICKS HIS CABINET.

★

THERE IS NOT A VOTER IN AMERICA THAT TWENTY-FOUR HOURS AFTER ANY SPEECH WAS MADE COULD REMEMBER TWO SENTENCES IN IT.

★

SHREWDNESS IN PUBLIC LIFE ALL OVER THE WORLD IS ALWAYS HONORED, WHILE HONESTY IN PUBLIC MEN IS GENERALLY ATTRIBUTED TO DUMBNESS AND IS SELDOM REWARDED.

★

OUR PUBLIC MEN TAKE THEMSELVES SO SERIOUS. IT JUST LOOKS LIKE THEY ARE STOOP-SHOULDERED FROM CARRYING OUR COUNTRY ON THEIR BACKS.

★

THE MORE I SEE OF POLITICS . . . THE MORE I WONDER WHAT IN THE WORLD ANY MAN WOULD EVER WANT TO TAKE IT UP FOR. THEN SOME PEOPLE WONDER WHY THE BEST MEN OF A COMMUNITY ARE NOT THE OFFICE HOLDERS.

★

EVERYBODY IS EXCITED OVER WHO WILL WIN THE ELECTION IN CHICAGO. THE SIDE WITH THE MOST MACHINE GUNS WILL WIN IT.

★

In this early day radio broadcast, Will Rogers' wife, Betty, is at his side while showgirls from the *Ziegfeld Follies* form the audience in this actual photo of a 1920s performance.

THE DEMOCRATS ARE HAVING A LOT OF FUN EXPOSING THE REPUBLICAN CAMPAIGN CORRUPTIONS, BUT THEY WOULD HAVE A LOT MORE FUN IF THEY KNEW WHERE THEY COULD LAY THEIR HANDS ON SOME OF IT THEMSELVES FOR NEXT NOVEMBER.

★

BEEN READING SUNDAY'S CASUALTY LISTS FROM AUTOMOBILES.
IT LOOKS LIKE EVERYBODY GETS RUN OVER BUT PRESIDENTIAL CANDIDATES.
IS THERE NO JUSTICE IN THE WORLD?

★

THE FARMERS STARVE THREE YEARS OUT OF FOUR BUT THE GOOD YEAR IS ALWAYS ELECTION YEAR. IT REALLY LOOKS LIKE THE LORD WAS IN CAHOOTS WITH THE REPUBLICANS, BUT IF HE IS THAT WOULD MAKE YOU ALMOST LOSE FAITH IN HIM.

★

NO ELEMENT, NO PARTY, NOT EVEN CONGRESS OR THE SENATE CAN HURT THIS COUNTRY NOW; IT'S TOO BIG. THAT'S WHY I CAN NEVER TAKE A POLITICIAN SERIOUSLY.

★

CONGRESS CAN PASS A BAD LAW AND AS SOON AS THE OLD NORMAL MAJORITY FINDS IT OUT THEY HAVE IT SCRATCHED OFF THE BOOK.

★

EVEN WHEN OUR NEXT WAR COMES, WE WILL THROUGH OUR SHORTSIGHTEDNESS NOT BE PREPARED BUT THAT WON'T BE ANYTHING FATAL. THE REAL ENERGY AND MINDS OF THE NORMAL MAJORITY WILL STEP IN AND HANDLE IT AND FIGHT IT THROUGH TO A SUCCESSFUL CONCLUSION.

★

THE COUNTRY IS NOT WHERE IT IS TODAY ON ACCOUNT OF ANY MAN. IT IS HERE ON ACCOUNT OF THE COMMON SENSE OF THE BIG NORMAL MAJORITY.

★

In his vaudeville and *Ziegfeld Follies* acts, trick roper Will Rogers would flip a lariat to tie knots.

A GENTLEMAN QUOTED ME ON THE FLOOR THE OTHER DAY. ANOTHER MEMBER TOOK EXCEPTION AND SAID HE OBJECTED TO THE REMARKS OF A PROFESSIONAL JOKE MAKER GOING INTO THE CONGRESSIONAL RECORD. THEY ARE THE PROFESSIONAL JOKE MAKERS. READ SOME OF THE BILLS THAT THEY HAVE PASSED, IF YOU THINK THEY AIN'T JOKE MAKERS. I COULD STUDY ALL MY LIFE AND NOT THINK UP HALF THE AMOUNT OF FUNNY THINGS THEY CAN THINK OF IN ONE SESSION OF CONGRESS. BESIDES, MY JOKES DON'T DO ANYBODY ANY HARM. YOU DON'T HAVE TO PAY ANY ATTENTION TO THEM. BUT EVERYONE OF THE JOKES THOSE BIRDS MAKE IS A LAW AND HURTS SOMEBODY (GENERALLY EVERYBODY). I OBJECT TO BEING CALLED A PROFESSIONAL. I AM AN AMATEUR BESIDE THEM.

THE TOWN WITH THE CHEAPEST LAND AND MOST CONCRETE CAN HAVE THE LARGEST STADIUM.

SO MUCH MONEY IS BEING SPENT ON THE CAMPAIGNS THAT I DOUBT IF EITHER MAN, AS GOOD AS THEY ARE, ARE WORTH WHAT IT WILL COST TO ELECT THEM.

NO NATION IN THE HISTORY OF THE WORLD WAS EVER SITTING AS PRETTY. IF WE WANT ANYTHING, ALL WE HAVE TO DO IS BUY IT ON CREDIT. SO THAT LEAVES US WITHOUT ANY ECONOMIC PROBLEM WHATEVER, EXCEPT PERHAPS SOME DAY TO HAVE TO PAY FOR THEM. BUT WE ARE CERTAINLY NOT THINKING ABOUT THAT THIS EARLY. YOURS FOR MORE CREDIT AND LONGER PAYMENTS.

Will Rogers in a movie-set still photo.

THERE IS ONE RULE THAT WORKS IN EVERY CALAMITY.
BE IT PESTILENCE, WAR OR FAMINE, THE RICH GET
RICHER AND POOR GET POORER.
THE POOR EVEN HELP ARRANGE IT.

THE ONE WAY TO DETECT A FEEBLE-MINDED MAN IS GET ONE ARGUING ON ECONOMICS.

ONE THING ABOUT FARMERS' RELIEF: IT CAN'T LAST LONG, FOR THE FARMERS AIN'T
GOT MUCH MORE TO BE RELIEVED OF.

DON'T MAKE THE FIRST PAYMENT ON ANYTHING. FIRST PAYMENTS IS WHAT
MADE US THINK WE WERE PROSPEROUS AND THE OTHER
NINETEEN IS WHAT SHOWED US WE WERE BROKE.

BIG BUSINESS DON'T GO BROKE ANY MORE. THE MINUTE IT LOOKS BAD FOR THEM,
THEY COMBINE WITH SOMETHING ELSE AND ISSUE MORE STOCK.

THIS OPEN-DOOR STUFF IS A LOT OF HOOEY. ANY DOOR IS ONLY OPEN TO THOSE THAT
HAVE THE BEST PRODUCT AT THE CHEAPEST MONEY.

AN ECONOMIST IS A MAN THAT CAN TELL YOU ANYTHING. HIS GUESS IS LIABLE TO BE
AS GOOD AS ANYBODY ELSE'S, TOO.

EVERY NATION MUST HAVE ITS LEGALIZED FORM OF GAMBLING.
WE HAVE OUR WALL STREET.

Will Rogers in a movie-set still photo with horses. He said, "Anyone who didn't like a horse—well, there's just something the matter with them."

IF WALL STREET PAID A TAX ON EVERY "GAME" THEY RUN, WE WOULD GET ENOUGH REVENUE TO RUN THE GOVERNMENT ON.

★

NO NATION HAS A MONOPOLY ON GOOD THINGS. EACH ONE HAS SOMETHING THAT THE OTHERS COULD WELL AFFORD TO ADOPT.

★

I GUESS OUR COUNTRY HOLDS THE RECORD FOR DUMBNESS. THE POPE SPOKE TO THE WORLD THIS MORNING IN THREE LANGUAGES AND WE DIDN'T UNDERSTAND A ONE OF 'EM. BUT THE MINUTE HE FINISHED AND THE LOCAL STATIONS GOT BACK TO SELLING CORN SALVE AND PYORRHEA TOOTH PASTE WE WERE RIGHT UP OUR INTELLECTUAL ALLEY AGAIN.

★

I SEE BY THE PAPERS THAT THEY SAY "GERMANY IS GOING INSANE." I WISH YOU COULD NAME ME A NATION THAT IS COMPETENT OF JUDGING INSANITY.

★

WHEN SOME NATION WANTS US TO HELP 'EM OUT THEY USE THE SAME OLD "GAG," THAT WE SHOULD EXERT OUR "MORAL LEADERSHIP" AND, LIKE A YAP, BELIEVE IT, WHEN, AS A MATTER OF TRUTH, NO NATION WANTS ANY OTHER NATION EXERTING A "MORAL LEADERSHIP" OVER 'EM EVEN IF THEY HAD ONE.

★

I DON'T CARE HOW LITTLE YOUR COUNTRY IS, YOU GOT A RIGHT TO RUN IT LIKE YOU WANT TO.

★

WHEN THE BIG NATIONS QUIT MEDDLING THEN THE WORLD WILL HAVE PEACE.

★

Will Rogers 1879·1935

I GUESS NO INDIVIDUAL EVER INVENTED CAN PASS THE BUCK
AS QUICK AS A NATION CAN.

★

IN SCHOOLS THEY HAVE WHAT THEY CALL INTELLIGENCE TESTS. WELL IF NATIONS HELD
'EM I DON'T BELIEVE WE WOULD BE WHAT YOU WOULD CALL A FAVORITE TO WIN IT.

★

ONE THING THAT WE DO WORSE THAN ANY OTHER NATION, IT IS TRY AND MANAGE
SOMEBODY ELSE'S AFFAIRS.

★

THERE'S THE ONE THING NO NATION CAN EVER ACCUSE US OF AND THAT IS SECRET
DIPLOMACY. OUR FOREIGN DEALINGS ARE AN OPEN BOOK. GENERALLY A CHECK BOOK.

★

NATIONS ARE JUST LIKE INDIVIDUALS. LOAN THEM MONEY AND YOU
LOSE THEIR FRIENDSHIP.

★

BEFORE YOU COMPLAIN, THINK OF PERU.

★

NO NATION EVER HAD TWO BETTER FRIENDS THAN WE HAVE. YOU KNOW WHO THEY
ARE? THE ATLANTIC AND PACIFIC OCEANS.

★

A BUNCH OF AMERICAN TOURISTS WERE HISSED AND STONED YESTERDAY IN FRANCE
BUT NOT UNTIL THEY HAD FINISHED BUYING.

★

WE WOULD NEVER UNDERSTAND WHY MEXICO WASN'T CRAZY ABOUT US. WE HAVE
ALWAYS HAD THEIR GOODWILL, OIL, COFFEE AND MINERALS AT HEART.

★

WOE BE TO A WEAK NATION IF THEY LIVE BY A STRONG ONE.

★

YOU CAN TAKE A SOB STORY AND A STICK OF CANDY AND LEAD AMERICA RIGHT OFF INTO THE DEAD SEA.

★

ONE GOOD THING ABOUT EUROPEAN NATIONS: THEY CAN'T HATE YOU SO BAD THEY WOULDN'T USE YOU.

★

HEADLINES IN THE PAPERS SAY: "EUROPE CRITICIZES U.S." IF MEMORY SERVES ME RIGHT WE HAVEN'T COMPLIMENTED THEM LATELY OURSELVES.

★

THERE IS NO INCOME TAX IN RUSSIA. BUT THERE'S NO INCOME.

★

DIPLOMATS ARE JUST AS ESSENTIAL TO STARTING A WAR AS SOLDIERS ARE FOR FINISHING IT. TAKE DIPLOMACY OUT OF A WAR AND THE THING WOULD FALL FLAT IN A WEEK.

★

I HAVE A SCHEME FOR STOPPING WAR. IT'S THIS—NO NATION IS ALLOWED TO ENTER A WAR TILL THEY HAVE PAID FOR THE LAST ONE.

★

WELL, THEY FINALLY STOPPED US FROM SENDING MARINES TO EVERY WAR THAT WE COULD HEAR OF. THEY ARE HAVING ONE IN AFGHANISTAN. THE THING WILL BE OVER BEFORE CONGRESS CAN PRONOUNCE IT, MUCH LESS FIND OUT WHERE IT IS LOCATED.

★

THE BEST OMEN OF INTERNATIONAL GOOD-WILL IS THAT CONFERENCES ARE GETTING SHORTER. NOW IF THEY WILL DO AWAY WITH 'EM ENTIRELY THERE WILL BE NO WAR.

★

Relaxing on the running board of his car between scenes on a movie set, Will Rogers studies a newspaper.

WARS WILL NEVER BE A SUCCESS UNTIL YOU HAVE A REFEREE AND UNTIL THEY ANNOUNCE BEFORE THEY START JUST WHAT IT'S FOR.

THERE IS ONLY ONE SURE WAY OF STOPPING WAR, THAT IS TO SEE THAT EVERY "STATESMAN" HAS THE SAME CHANCE TO REFLECT AFTER IT'S OVER THAT THESE BOYS MAKING "POPPIES" HAVE HAD.

WAR TALK IN EUROPE HAS PRETTY NEAR DIED OUT ON ACCOUNT OF NO INTERNA-TIONAL CONFERENCES BEING HELD. THEY HAVEN'T GOT MUCH CHANCE OF GETTING SORE AT EACH OTHER.

NATIONS WILL GIVE UP THEIR LIVES (EVEN CHEER ABOUT IT). THEY WILL GIVE UP THEIR MONEY IN ORDER TO GIVE UP THEIR LIVES, BUT TO ASK ONE TO GIVE UP THEIR TRADE TO PREVENT A WAR, WELL, THAT HAS NEVER BEEN DONE.

THE DIFFERENCE BETWEEN A BANDIT AND A PATRIOT IS A GOOD PRESS AGENT.

WE ONLY HAVE ONE OR TWO WARS IN A LIFETIME. BUT WE HAVE THREE MEALS A DAY. WHEN YOU HAVE HELPED RAISE THE STANDARD OF COOKING THEN YOU WOULD HAVE RAISED THE ONLY THING IN THE WORLD THAT MATTERS.

Publicity photos of Will Rogers.

THERE HAS BEEN WAR SINCE THE BEGINNING OF TIME AND WE ARE NO SMARTER THAN THE PEOPLE THAT HAVE GONE BEFORE US. THERE IS APT TO BE SOME MORE WAR.

★

EVERY WAR HAS BEEN PRECEDED BY A PEACE CONFERENCE. THAT'S WHAT ALWAYS STARTS THE NEXT WAR.

★

ASKING EUROPE TO DISARM IS LIKE ASKING A MAN IN CHICAGO TO GIVE UP HIS LIFE INSURANCE.

★

PEOPLE TALK PEACE BUT MEN GIVE THEIR LIFE'S WORK TO WAR. IT WON'T STOP 'TIL THERE IS AS MUCH BRAINS AND SCIENTIFIC STUDY PUT TO AID PEACE AS THERE IS TO PROMOTE WAR.

★

WHEN YOU GET INTO TROUBLE FIVE THOUSAND MILES FROM HOME YOU'VE GOT TO HAVE BEEN LOOKING FOR IT.

★

IT TAKES QUITE A SENSE OF HUMOR FOR THESE PEOPLE TO UNDERSTAND US SHAKING HANDS WITH ONE HAND AND SHOOTING WITH THE OTHER.

★

THERE IS NOTHING THAT MAKES A NATION OR AN INDIVIDUAL AS MAD AS TO HAVE SOMEBODY SAY, "NOW THIS IS REALLY NONE OF MY BUSINESS BUT I AM JUST ADVISING YOU." IF I SLEEP WITH A GUN UNDER MY PILLOW, I DON'T WANT SOMEBODY FROM ACROSS THE STREET TO "ADVISE" ME THAT I DON'T NEED IT.

★

During his vaudeville era, Will looped a lariat while riding a unicycle, and it inspired this cartoon.

DRAFT CAPITAL AS WELL AS MEN. BOYS, THERE AIN'T GOING TO BE NO WAR.

★

DIPLOMATS ARE JUST AS ESSENTIAL TO STARTING A WAR AS SOLDIERS ARE FOR FINISHING IT.

★

EUROPE WONDERED HOW AMERICA COULD TRAIN MEN SO QUICKLY. WELL, WHEN YOU ONLY HAVE TO TRAIN THEM TO GO ONE WAY YOU CAN DO IT IN HALF THE TIME.

★

HERE WE GO AGAIN! AMERICA IS RUNNING TRUE TO FORM, FIXING SOME OTHER COUNTRY'S BUSINESS FOR 'EM JUST AS WE ALWAYS DO. WE MEAN WELL, BUT WILL WIND UP IN WRONG AS USUAL.

★

WE HAVE KILLED MORE PEOPLE CELEBRATING OUR INDEPENDENCE THAN WE LOST FIGHTING FOR IT. WE WOULD CELEBRATE THE ENDING OF EACH OF OUR WARS BUT WE HAVEN'T GOT ENOUGH PEOPLE TO GO AROUND.

★

A TAX PAID ON THE DAY YOU BUY IS NOT AS TOUGH AS ASKING YOU FOR IT THE NEXT YEAR WHEN YOU ARE BROKE.

★

WE HAVE IT ON THE BEST OF OUR INFORMATION THAT TAXES WILL BE RELIEVED, BUT NOT UNTIL AFTER YOUR DEATH.

★

IF NOBODY WANTS TO DISARM WITH US, WE WILL SHOW 'EM WE ARE RIGHT. WE WILL SHAME 'EM INTO IT—IF WE HAVE TO SINK OUR LAST LIFE PRESERVER TO DO IT.

★

Will Rogers twirls a crinoline around a baseball team.

THE GOOD OLD DAYS WITH MOST OF US WAS WHEN WE DIDN'T EARN ENOUGH TO PAY AN INCOME TAX.

★

CONGRESS HAS PASSED THE BIG INHERITANCE TAX. THAT GETS YOU WHEN YOU'RE GONE. I THINK IT'S A GOOD LAW. YOU HAD HAD THE USE OF THE MONEY DURING YOUR LIFETIME, SO TURN IT OVER TO THE GOVERNMENT AND THEY CAN DO SOME DARN FOOL THINGS WITH IT. MAYBE AS FOOLISH AS THE CHILDREN OF THE DECEASED WOULD. IT'S ONLY ONE GENERATION FROM A PICK HANDLE TO A PUTTER AND ONE MORE FROM A TUXEDO TO A TRAMP.

★

THEY GOT SUCH A HIGH INHERITANCE TAX ON 'EM THAT YOU WON'T CATCH THESE OLD RICH BOYS DYING PROMISCUOUSLY LIKE THEY DID. THIS BILL MAKES PATRIOTS OUT OF EVERYBODY. YOU SURE DO DIE FOR YOUR COUNTRY IF YOU DIE FROM NOW ON.

★

PEOPLE WANT JUST TAXES MORE THAN THEY WANT LOWER TAXES. THEY WANT TO KNOW THAT EVERY MAN IS PAYING HIS PROPORTIONATE SHARE ACCORDING TO HIS WEALTH.

★

WHEN A PARTY CAN'T THINK OF ANYTHING ELSE THEY ALWAYS FALL BACK ON LOWER TAXES. IT HAS A MAGIC SOUND TO A VOTER JUST LIKE FAIRYLAND IS SPOKEN OF AND DREAMED OF BY CHILDREN. BUT NO CHILD HAS EVER SEEN IT. NEITHER HAS ANY VOTER EVER LIVED TO SEE THE DAY WHEN HIS TAXES WERE LOWERED.

★

THERE IS A TREMENDOUS MOVEMENT ON TO GET LOWER TAXES ON EARNED INCOME. THEN WILL COME THE REAL PROBLEM. WHO AMONG US ON SALARY ARE EARNING OUR INCOME?

WE DON'T SEEM TO BE ABLE TO EVEN CHECK CRIME. WHY NOT LEGALIZE IT AND PUT A HEAVY TAX ON IT. MAKE THE TAX FOR ROBBERY SO HIGH THAT A BANDIT COULDN'T AFFORD TO ROB ANYONE UNLESS HE HAD A LOT OF DOUGH. WE HAVE TAXED OTHER INDUSTRIES OUT OF BUSINESS, IT MIGHT WORK HERE.

THE IDEA THAT A TAX ON SOMETHING KEEPS ANYBODY FROM BUYING IT IS A LOT OF "HOOEY." THEY PUT IT ON GASOLINE ALL OVER THE COUNTRY AND IT HASN'T KEPT A SOUL AT HOME A SINGLE NIGHT OR DAY. YOU COULD PUT A DOLLAR A GALLON ON AND STILL A PEDESTRIAN COULDN'T CROSS THE STREET WITH SAFETY WITHOUT ARMOR.

PUT A GOOD TAX ON BEER AND THAT WOULD TAKE CARE OF THE UNEMPLOYMENT FUND.

★

THE INCOME TAX HAS MADE MORE LIARS OUT OF THE AMERICAN PEOPLE THAN GOLF HAS.

★

IT'S A GREAT COUNTRY BUT YOU CAN'T LIVE IN IT FOR NOTHING.

★

COMEDIANS HAVEN'T IMPROVED. NOTHING HAS IMPROVED BUT TAXES.

★

I SEE A GOOD DEAL OF TALK FROM WASHINGTON ABOUT LOWERING THE TAXES. I HOPE THEY DO GET 'EM LOWERED DOWN ENOUGH SO PEOPLE CAN AFFORD TO PAY 'EM.

YOU ARE GOING TO NEED SALES TAXES, BOTH FEDERAL AND STATE, INCOME TAX, AND A LOT OF OTHER KINDS. IT'S A GREAT COUNTRY BUT YOU CAN'T LIVE IN IT FOR NOTHING.

★

THE CRIME OF TAXATION IS NOT IN THE TAKING OF IT, IT'S IN THE WAY THAT IT'S SPENT.

★

WE ARE A FUNNY PEOPLE. WE ELECT OUR PRESIDENTS, BE THEY REPUBLICAN OR DEMOCRAT, THEN GO HOME AND START DARING 'EM TO MAKE GOOD.

★

THEY SAY WASHINGTON NEVER WAS AS DRY. COURSE YOU GOT TO LAY MOST OF THAT TO THE SENATE AND CONGRESS NOT BEING IN SESSION.

★

YOU KNOW STATISTICS HAVE PROVEN THAT LISTENING TO PROHIBITION LECTURERS HAS DRIVEN MORE PEOPLE TO DRINK THAN ANY OTHER CAUSE.

★

I AM KIND OF LIKE A POLITICIAN. THE LESS I KNOW ABOUT ANYTHING THE MORE I CAN SAY ABOUT IT.

★

WINNING A STRAW VOTE IS LIKE BEATING YOURSELF AT SOLITAIRE.

★

THERE IS NOTHING AS SHORT-SIGHTED AS A POLITICIAN.

★

LINCOLN HAS HAD MORE PUBLIC MEN SPEAK OF HIS GOOD QUALITIES, AND FEW COPY ANY OF THEM, THAN ANY MAN AMERICA EVER PRODUCED.

★

ONE PECULIAR THING ABOUT A DEMOCRAT, HE WOULD RATHER HAVE APPLAUSE THAN SALARY.

★

Will Rogers: polo player with a three-goal handicap.

THERE IS SOMETHING ABOUT A REPUBLICAN POLITICIAN, THEY ARE SMART BUT THEY JUST DON'T KNOW MUCH.

★

OVER HOME A CONGRESSMAN IS NEVER ANY BETTER THAN HIS ROADS.

★

IF I SAY SOMETHING WRONG, I CAN ALWAYS COME CLEAR BY SAYING I THOUGHT I WAS A SENATOR.

★

CONGRESS WOULD AMEND THE TEN COMMANDMENTS IF THEY EVER READ THEM. AS A JOKE-MAKER, CONGRESS PUTS ME IN THE CLASS OF THE AMATEUR.

★

WE JUST AS WELL BECOME RECONCILED TO THE FACT THAT THE OLD POLITICIAN IS WITH US "EVEN UNTO DEATH."

★

TOO BAD OUR SYSTEM OF ETIQUETTE DON'T ALLOW EVERYBODY TO SPEAK THE WHOLE TRUTH WHILE THEY ARE IN OFFICE.

★

IT COSTS TEN TIMES MORE TO GOVERN US THAN IT USED TO, AND WE ARE NOT GOVERNED ONE-TENTH AS GOOD.

★

I LOVE A DOG, HE DOES NOTHING FOR POLITICAL REASONS.

★

EVERYDAY LIFE

ANYBODY WHOSE PLEASURE IS WATCHING SOMEBODY ELSE DIE IS ABOUT AS LITTLE USE TO HUMANITY AS THE PERSON BEING ELECTROCUTED.

★

YOU MUST JUDGE A MAN'S GREATNESS BY HOW MUCH HE WILL BE MISSED.

★

PEOPLE ARE MARVELOUS IN THEIR GENEROSITY IF THEY JUST KNOW THE CAUSE IS THERE.

★

IT'S GREAT TO BE GREAT, BUT IT'S GREATER TO BE HUMAN.

★

INDIANS AND PRIMITIVE RACES WERE THE HIGHEST CIVILIZED BECAUSE THEY WERE MORE SATISFIED AND THEY DEPENDED LESS ON EACH OTHER AND TOOK LESS FROM EACH OTHER.

NOTHING MAKES A MAN BROAD-MINDED LIKE ADVERSITY.

THE MINUTE A FELLOW GETS INTO THE CHAMBER OF COMMERCE, HE QUITS MOWING HIS OWN LAWN.

I CAN REMEMBER WHEN A MAN COULD BE CONSIDERED RESPECTABLE WITHOUT BELONGING TO A GOLF CLUB.

IT'S NOT WHAT YOU PAY A MAN BUT WHAT HE COSTS YOU THAT COUNTS.

A MAN IN THE COUNTRY DOES HIS OWN THINKING. GET HIM INTO TOWN AND HE WILL BE THINKING SECOND-HANDED.

Will Rogers as an after-dinner speaker.

THE LORD SO CONSTI-TUTED EVERYBODY THAT NO MATTER WHAT COLOR YOU ARE, YOU REQUIRE THE SAME AMOUNT OF NOURISHMENT.

★

CITIES ARE LIKE GENTLEMEN. THEY ARE BORN NOT MADE.

★

GREAT ARTISTS SAY THAT THE MOST BEAUTIFUL THING IN THE WORLD IS A BABY. WELL, THE NEXT IS AN OLD LADY, FOR EVERY WRINKLE IS A PICTURE.

★

THERE IS NO LESS SICKNESS, NO LESS EARTHQUAKES, NO LESS PROGRESS, NO LESS INVENTIONS, NO LESS MORALITY, NO LESS CHRISTIANITY UNDER ONE THAN THE OTHER. THEY ARE ALL THE SAME. IT WON'T MAKE 50 CENTS DIFFERENCE TO A ONE OF YOU. UNLESS YOU'RE FOOLISH ENOUGH TO BET ON IT.

★

CALL ME A "RUBE" AND A "HICK," BUT I'D LOT RATHER BE THE MAN WHO BOUGHT THE BROOKLYN BRIDGE THAN THE MAN WHO SOLD IT.

★

THE MORE YOU KNOW THE MORE YOU THINK SOMEBODY OWES YOU A LIVING.

★

THE TIME AIN'T FAR OFF WHEN A WOMAN WON'T KNOW ANY MORE THAN A MAN.

★

IF YOU LIVE LIFE RIGHT, DEATH IS A JOKE AS FAR AS FEAR IS CONCERNED.

★

Betty and Will Rogers watch an at-home performance by (left to right) Jim, Mary and Will Jr.

EDUCATION NEVER HELPED MORALS. THE MOST SAVAGE PEOPLE ARE THE MOST MORAL. THE SMARTER THE GUY THE BIGGER THE RASCAL.

★

THE HIGHER THE EDUCATION THE HIGHER PRICED DRINKS THEY BECOME ACCUSTOMED TO. PROHIBITION WILL NEVER CATCH UP WITH EDUCATION.

★

THE LORD SPLIT KNOWLEDGE UP AMONG HIS SUBJECTS ABOUT EQUAL. THE SO-CALLED IGNORANT IS HAPPY. YOU THINK HE IS HAPPY BECAUSE HE DON'T KNOW ANY BETTER. MAYBE HE IS HAPPY BECAUSE HE KNOWS ENOUGH TO BE HAPPY. THE SMART ONE KNOWS A LOT. THAT MAKES HIM UNHAPPY BECAUSE HE CAN'T IMPART IT TO HIS FRIENDS. DISCONTENT COMES IN PROPORTION TO KNOWLEDGE.

★

NO MAN CAN BE CONDEMNED FOR OWNING A DOG. AS LONG AS HE'S GOT A DOG HE'S GOT A FRIEND AND THE POORER HE GETS THE BETTER FRIEND HE HAS.

★

WHAT ALL OF US KNOW PUT TOGETHER DON'T MEAN ANYTHING. NOTHING DON'T MEAN ANYTHING. WE ARE HERE FOR A SPELL AND PASS ON. ANYONE WHO THINKS THAT CIVILIZATION HAS ADVANCED IS AN EGOTIST.

★

FORDS AND BATHTUBS HAVE YOU AND CLEANED YOU. BUT YOU WERE JUST AS IGNORANT WHEN YOU GOT THERE. WE KNOW A LOT OF THINGS WE USED TO DIDN'T KNOW BUT WE DON'T KNOW ANY WAY TO PREVENT 'EM HAPPENING.

★

Ziegfeld Follies publicity photo of Will Rogers ringing the cast with a crinoline.

EVERYBODY IS IGNO-
RANT. ONLY ON
DIFFERENT SUBJECTS.

★

WHEN IGNORANCE GETS STARTED, IT KNOWS NO BOUNDS.

★

THERE IS NOTHING AS EASY AS DENOUNCING. IT DON'T TAKE MUCH TO SEE THAT SOMETHING IS WRONG BUT IT DOES TAKE SOME EYESIGHT TO SEE WHAT WILL PUT IT RIGHT AGAIN.

★

NOWADAYS IT IS ABOUT AS BIG A CRIME TO BE DUMB AS IT IS TO BE DISHONEST.

★

THE AMERICAN PEOPLE ARE A VERY GENEROUS PEOPLE AND WILL FORGIVE ALMOST ANY WEAKNESS, WITH THE POSSIBLE EXCEPTION OF STUPIDITY.

★

YOU CAN'T LEGISLATE INTELLIGENCE AND COMMON SENSE INTO PEOPLE. YOU CAN'T BROADEN A MAN'S VISION IF HE WASN'T BORN WITH ONE.

★

HUMANITY IS NOT YET READY FOR EITHER REAL TRUTH OR REAL HARMONY.

★

A FANATIC IS ALWAYS THE FELLOW THAT IS ON THE OPPOSITE SIDE.

★

A MAN CAN FOOL YOU WITH HIS MIND, AND HIS SOUL AND HIS HEART, BUT IF YOU FOLLOW HIS FEET YOU WILL PRETTY NEAR FIND OUT WHERE HE IS GOING.

★

Ready to play polo, Will leads his horse to the field he constructed at his Santa Monica ranch.

NOTHING WILL SPOIL A BIG MAN'S LIFE LIKE TOO MUCH TRUTH.

HALF OUR LIFE IS SPENT TRYING TO FIND SOMETHING TO DO WITH THE TIME WE HAVE RUSHED THROUGH LIFE TRYING TO SAVE.

★

A THING THAT IS FREE IS OF NO EARTHLY IMPORTANCE.

★

NOTHING AS STUPID AS AN EDUCATED MAN IF YOU GET HIM OFF THE THING HE WAS EDUCATED ON.

★

NOBODY WANTS HIS CAUSE NEAR AS BAD AS HE WANTS TO TALK ABOUT HIS CAUSE.

★

THIS THING OF BEING A HERO, ABOUT THE MAIN THING TO DO IS TO KNOW WHEN TO DIE. PROLONGED LIFE HAS RUINED MORE MEN THAN IT EVER MADE.

★

MODERN HISTORY HAS PROVEN THAT THERE HAS NEVER BEEN A WILL LEFT THAT WAS CARRIED OUT EXACTLY AS THE MAKER OF THE MONEY INTENDED.

★

NOTHING MAKES PEOPLE MORE ALIKE THAN PUTTING A DRESS SUIT ON 'EM.

★

ACTUAL KNOWLEDGE OF THE FUTURE WAS NEVER LOWER, BUT HOPE WAS NEVER HIGHER. CONFIDENCE WILL BEAT PREDICTIONS ANY TIME.

★

ALL WE HEAR IS "WHAT'S THE MATTER WITH THE COUNTRY?" "WHAT'S THE MATTER WITH THE WORLD?" THERE AIN'T BUT ONE THING WRONG WITH EVERY ONE OF US IN THE WORLD, AND THAT'S SELFISHNESS.

★

Will Rogers demonstrates one of his equestrian lariat skills.

THE FELLOW SITTING OFF LOOKING AT YOU CAN TELL BETTER HOW YOU ARE DOING AND WHAT YOUR PROSPECTS ARE THAN YOU CAN YOURSELF.

HISTORY AIN'T WHAT IT IS. IT'S WHAT SOME WRITER WANTED IT TO BE.

THERE NEVER WAS SUCH A DEMAND FOR SPEED, FOR LESS REASON. THERE IS NOT A ONE OF US THAT COULDN'T WALK WHERE WE ARE GOING AND THEN GET THERE EARLIER THAN WE HAVE ANY BUSINESS.

THEORIES ARE GREAT, THEY SOUND GREAT, BUT THE MINUTE YOU ARE ASKED TO PROVE ONE IN ACTUAL LIFE, WHY THE THING BLOWS UP.

THE WORLD IS FULL OF MEN WHO DO BIG THINGS, BUT WHEN YOU MEET 'EM THEY ARE NOT OUTSTANDING PERSONALITIES. PRETTY NEAR EVERYBODY IS ALMOST ALIKE.

YOU CAN LOOK AT HALF THE GUY'S STOMACHS IN THE WORLD, AND YOU CAN SEE THEY DON'T KNOW HOW TO ORDER FOR THEMSELVES.

I CERTAINLY KNOW THAT A COMEDIAN CAN ONLY LAST TILL HE EITHER TAKES HIMSELF SERIOUS OR HIS AUDIENCE TAKES HIM SERIOUS, AND I DON'T WANT EITHER ONE OF THOSE TO HAPPEN TO ME TILL I AM DEAD (IF THEN).

★

Lobby card for the 1933 Fox picture *State Fair,* starring Will Rogers with Janet Gaynor as his romantic daughter. *Courtesy of the Gordon Kuntz collection.*

I GUESS THERE IS NO TWO RACES OF PEOPLE IN WORSE REPUTE WITH EVERYBODY THAN THE INTERNATIONAL BANKERS AND THE FOLKS THAT PUT ALL THOSE PINS IN NEW SHIRTS.

★

I THINK THE SAME FELLOW WHO STARTED THAT SELF-MADE MAN GAG STARTED THAT OTHER ASININE EXPRESSION, "100 PER CENT AMERICAN." EVERY HUMAN FROM THE TIME HE IS WEANED IS SELF-MADE. AND HOW DO YOU KNOW WHEN A MAN IS MADE ANYHOW? HE MAY BE ONLY PARTLY FINISHED WHEN A LOT OF GUYS CALL HIM MADE.

★

YOU CAN'T HAVE A PICNIC UNLESS THE PARTY CARRYING THE BASKET COMES.

★

POPULARITY IS THE EASIEST THING IN THE WORLD TO GAIN AND IT IS THE HARDEST THING TO HOLD.

★

RUMOR TRAVELS FASTER BUT IT DON'T STAY PUT AS LONG AS TRUTH.

★

AIN'T BUT ONE THING WRONG WITH EVERY ONE OF US IN THE WORLD AND THAT'S SELFISHNESS.

★

EVERYBODY LIKES TO HEAR IT STRAIGHT FROM THE BOSS, EVEN IF YOU ARE GOING TO GET FIRED.

★

IF YOU WANT TO SHIP OFF FAT BEEF CATTLE AT THE END OF THEIR EXISTENCE, YOU HAVE GOT TO HAVE 'EM SATISFIED ON THE RANGE.

★

WHEN YOU STRADDLE A THING, IT TAKES A LONG TIME TO EXPLAIN IT.

★

I HOPE WE NEVER SEE THE DAY WHEN A THING IS AS BAD AS SOME OF OUR NEWSPAPERS MAKE IT.

★

THERE IS A GREAT TENDENCY ALL OVER THE COUNTRY NOW TO BE HIGH BROW. MORE PEOPLE SHOULD WORK FOR THEIR DINNER INSTEAD OF DRESSING FOR IT.

★

WELL, THE XMAS SPIRIT IS OVER NOW. EVERYBODY CAN GET BACK TO THEIR NATURAL DISPOSITIONS. IF THERE HAD BEEN AS MANY GOOD WISHES IN THE HEART AS THERE WAS ON PAPER THE DEVIL WOULD HAVE TO DIG UP SOME NEW CLIENTS.

★

HUNGER DOESN'T NEED MUCH ENCOURAGEMENT. IT JUST KEEPS COMING AROUND NATURALLY.

★

THE FOOTBALL SEASON IS ABOUT OVER. EDUCATION NEVER HAD A MORE FINANCIAL YEAR. SCHOOL WILL COMMENCE NOW.

★

BANKING AND AFTER DINNER SPEAKING ARE TWO OF THE MOST NON-ESSENTIAL INDUSTRIES WE HAVE IN THIS COUNTRY. I AM READY TO REFORM IF THEY ARE.

★

NOTHING BREAKS UP HOMES, COUNTRY AND NATIONS LIKE SOMEBODY PUBLISHING THEIR MEMOIRS.

★

WHOEVER WROTE THE TEN COMMANDMENTS MADE 'EM SHORT. THEY MAY NOT ALWAYS BE KEPT BUT THEY CAN BE UNDERSTOOD.

★

Will Rogers reads a newspaper and twirls a rope in tandem.

NEVER WAS A NATION FOUNDED AND MAINTAINED WITHOUT SOME KIND OF BELIEF IN SOMETHING AND THAT IS RELIGION. NEVER MIND WHAT KIND. BUT IT'S GOT TO BE SOMETHING OR YOU WILL FAIL AT THE FINISH.

★

STATISTICS HAVE PROVEN THAT THERE ARE TWENTY-FIVE BATHTUBS SOLD TO EVERY BIBLE.

★

THERE IS NO ARGUMENT IN THE WORLD CARRIES THE HATRED THAT A RELIGIOUS BELIEF ONE DOES. THE MORE LEARNED A MAN IS THE LESS CONSIDERATION HE HAS FOR ANOTHER MAN'S BELIEF.

★

I BET ANY SUNDAY COULD BE MADE AS POPULAR AT CHURCH AS EASTER IS IF YOU MADE 'EM FASHION SHOWS TOO. THE AUDIENCE IS SO BUSY LOOKING AT EACH OTHER THAT THE PREACHER JUST AS WELL RECITE GUNGA DIN.

★

I WAS RAISED PREDOMINANTLY A METHODIST BUT I HAVE TRAVELED SO MUCH, MIXED WITH SO MANY PEOPLE IN ALL PARTS OF THE WORLD, I DON'T KNOW JUST NOW WHAT I AM. I KNOW I HAVE NEVER BEEN A NON BELIEVER. BUT I CAN HONESTLY TELL YOU THAT I DON'T THINK THAT ANY ONE RELIGION IS THE RELIGION.

★

EVERY MAN'S RELIGION IS GOOD. THERE IS NONE OF IT BAD. WE ARE ALL TRYING TO ARRIVE AT THE SAME PLACE ACCORDING TO OUR OWN CONSCIENCE AND TEACHINGS. IT DON'T MATTER WHICH ROAD YOU TAKE.

Publicity photo of Will Rogers.

★

DEATH KNOWS NO DENOMINATION. DEATH DRAWS NO COLOR LINE.

★

THE MINISTRY IN ALL DENOMINATIONS ARE THE POOREST PAID WORKERS IN THE WORLD. THEY WOULD FORM A UNION AND DEMAND MORE PAY, BUT THEY DON'T GET ENOUGH TO PAY DUES INTO A UNION SO THEY CAN'T FORM ONE.

★

A WIFE IS THE CHEAPEST THING YOU CAN GET IN THE LONG RUN IN THE FEMALE LINE.

★

THEY WERE VERY RELIGIOUS PEOPLE THAT COME OVER HERE FROM THE OLD COUNTRY. THEY WERE VERY HUMAN. THEY WOULD SHOOT A COUPLE OF INDIANS ON THEIR WAY TO EVERY PRAYER MEETING.

★

I DOUBT IF A CHARGING ELEPHANT, OR A RHINO, IS AS DETERMINED OR HARD TO CHECK AS A SOCIALLY AMBITIOUS MOTHER.

Will Rogers prepares for a flight in an open-cockpit biplane.

"DIVORCES IN RENO HAVE INCREASED OVER 105 PER CENT IN THE LAST YEAR." NOW, THAT'S PROSPERITY, FOR YOU CAN'T BE BROKE AND GET A DIVORCE. THAT'S WHY THE POOR HAVE TO LIVE WITH EACH OTHER. THERE IS NOTHING THAT DENOTES PROSPERITY QUICKER THAN TO HEAR THAT "SO AND SO AND HIS WIFE AIN'T GETTING ALONG."

★

GOLF IS THE ONLY GAME IN THE WORLD WHERE IT TAKES LONGER TO EXPLAIN THAN IT DOES TO PLAY.

★

THERE IS NOTHING EFFEMINATE ABOUT THIS GOLF THING AS PLAYED BY THESE CHAMPION WOMEN.

★

I DON'T THINK I EVER HURT ANY MAN'S FEELINGS BY MY LITTLE GAGS. I KNOW I NEVER WILLFULLY DID IT. WHEN I HAVE TO DO THAT TO MAKE A LIVING, I WILL QUIT.

★

BASEBALL IS IN FOR A GREAT YEAR. IT'S OUR NATIONAL GAME AND WILL ALWAYS BE OUR NATIONAL GAME. WE BECOME A GREAT NATION UNDER BASEBALL AND COMMENCED TO FLOP THE MINUTE WE STARTED TO TAKE UP A LOT OF POOR SUBSTITUTES.

★

THE FOOTBALL SEASON IS CLOSING AND COLLEGE LIFE IS ABOUT OVER FOR THE YEAR. A FEW STUDENTS WILL STAY OUT THE SEASON FOR THE DANCES, AND SOME OF THE PLAYERS MAY TAKE UP A COUPLE OF PIPE COURSES AND HANG AROUND TILL SPRING PRACTICE STARTS, BUT MOST OF THE GOOD ONES WILL GO HOME FOR THE WINTER TO SHOW THE CLIPPINGS.

★

WHEN IN DOUBT, TELL A FUNNY 'TIL YOU SEE WHAT THE OTHER FELLOW IS GOING TO DO.

★

MAKE EVERY SPEAKER AS SOON AS HE TELLS ALL HE KNOWS, SIT DOWN. THAT WILL SHORTEN OUR SPEECHES SO MUCH YOU WILL BE OUT BY LUNCH TIME.

★

TERRIBLE TO HAVE A LAW TELLING YOU YOU GOT TO DO SOMETHING. BUT YOU AIN'T GOING TO DO IT UNLESS THERE IS.

★

PERSONALLY I DON'T THINK YOU CAN MAKE A LAWYER HONEST BY AN ACT OF THE LEGISLATURE. YOU'VE GOT TO WORK ON HIS CONSCIENCE. AND HIS LACK OF A CONSCIENCE IS WHAT MAKES HIM A LAWYER.

★

IF IT WASN'T FOR WILLS, LAWYERS WOULD HAVE TO GO TO WORK AT AN ESSENTIAL EMPLOYMENT.

Will Rogers and artist Charles Russell on a movie set in Hollywood.

Facing: Will Rogers in his famous narrow-brim Stetson, holding a lariat.

ONLY ONE WAY YOU CAN BEAT A LAWYER IN A DEATH CASE. THAT IS TO DIE WITH NOTHING.

★

ALL DOCTORS SHOULD MAKE ENOUGH OUT OF THOSE WHO ARE WELL ABLE TO PAY TO BE ABLE TO DO ALL WORK FOR THE POOR FREE. ONE THING THAT A POOR PERSON SHOULD NEVER BE EXPECTED TO PAY FOR IS MEDICAL ATTENTION AND NOT FROM AN ORGANIZED CHARITY BUT FROM OUR BEST DOCTORS. YOUR DOCTOR BILL SHOULD BE PAID LIKE YOUR INCOME TAX, ACCORDING TO WHAT YOU HAVE.

★

BEST DOCTOR IN THE WORLD IS THE VETERINARIAN. HE CAN'T ASK HIS PATIENTS WHAT'S THE MATTER. HE'S JUST GOT TO KNOW.

★

WHEN A DOCTOR HAS PULLED YOU THROUGH WHY YOU ALWAYS GOT A WARM PLACE IN YOUR HEART FOR HIM.

★

THERE IS NOTHING THAT KEEPS POOR PEOPLE POOR AS MUCH AS PAYING DOCTOR BILLS.

★

PARADES SHOULD BE CLASSED AS A NUISANCE AND PARTICIPANTS SHOULD BE SUBJECT TO A TERM IN PRISON. EVEN THE PEOPLE IN THEM HATE THEM.

★

THINK UP SOMETHING FOR YOUR TOWN TO CELEBRATE. HAVE A PARADE. AMERICANS LIKE TO PARADE. WE ARE A PARADING NATION. "UPLURIBUS PARADITORIOUS" (SOME PARADERS).

★

Will Rogers with "Sheriff" Buck McKee on Teddy, teamed in a vaudeville trick-roping routine.

WHEN A FELLOW DON'T HAVE MUCH MIND IT DON'T TAKE HIM LONG TO MAKE IT UP.

★

TWO THINGS THAT TICKLE THE FANCY OF OUR CITIZENS, ONE IS LET THEM ACT ON A COMMITTEE, AND THE OTHER IS TO PROMISE TO LET HIM WALK IN A PARADE. WHAT AMERICA NEEDS IS MORE MILEAGE OUT OF OUR PARADES.

★

YOU WOULD BE SURPRISED WHAT THERE IS TO SEE IN THIS GREAT COUNTRY WITHIN 200 MILES OF WHERE ANY OF US LIVE. I DON'T CARE WHAT STATE OR WHAT TOWN.

★

IF WE REALLY WANTED TO HONOR OUR BOYS, WHY DIDN'T WE LET THEM SIT ON THE REVIEWING STANDS AND MAKE THE PEOPLE MARCH THOSE FIFTEEN MILES? THEY DIDN'T WANT TO PARADE, THEY WANTED TO GO HOME AND REST.

★

HISTORY WILL RECORD: "AMERICA, A NATION THAT FLOURISHED FROM 1900 TO 1942, CONCEIVED MANY ODD INVENTIONS TO GETTING SOMEWHERE, BUT COULD THINK OF NOTHING TO DO WHEN THEY GOT THERE."

★

TROUBLE WITH AMERICAN TRANSPORTATION IS THAT YOU CAN GET SOMEWHERE QUICKER THAN YOU CAN THINK OF A REASON FOR GOING THERE. WHAT WE NEED NOW IS A NEW EXCUSE TO GO SOMEWHERE.

★

WHAT THE YOUTH NEED IS NARROWER PANTS LEGS AND BROADER IDEAS.

★

WHAT WE NEED IS CLEANER MINDS AND DIRTIER FINGER NAILS.

★

IF GOLF WAS PLAYED AS MUCH AS IT WAS TALKED IT WOULD SUPPLANT POKER AS OUR NATIONAL GAME.

★

THERE IS MORE PEOPLE LOOKING FOR PARKING PLACES THAN THERE IS FOR JOBS.

★

ANYTHING IS JUST AS GOOD AS THE HEAD OF IT AND NO BETTER.

★

LIFE INSURANCE IS A GREAT THING. IT'S THE ONLY WAY WE HAVE OF BEING REMEMBERED AFTER WE ARE GONE. THE EXTENT OF YOUR MEMORY DEPENDS ON HOW LONG THE MONEY LASTS.

★

DON'T GAMBLE. TAKE ALL YOUR SAVINGS AND BUY SOME GOOD STOCK. IF IT DON'T GO UP DON'T BUY IT.

★

IF THEY ARE GOING TO ARGUE RELIGION IN THE CHURCH INSTEAD OF TEACHING IT, NO WONDER YOU SEE MORE PEOPLE AT A CIRCUS THAN AT A CHURCH.

★

★

ADVICE CAN GET YOU INTO MORE TROUBLE THAN A GUN CAN.

★

THERE ARE CERTAIN THINGS IN THIS LIFE WE HAVE BECOME ACCUSTOMED TO KNOW
THAT WE CAN DEPEND ON. THEY NEVER FAIL. WE CAN ALWAYS DEPEND ON A PUNC-
TURE IF THERE IS NO SPARE TIRE—YOUR INSURANCE BEING DUE JUST WHEN EVERY-
THING ELSE IS—AN AFTER-DINNER SPEAKER SAYING, "IT'S GROWING LATE AND I
WILL TRY AND MAKE IT BRIEF."

★

YOU DON'T CLIMB OUT OF ANYTHING AS QUICK AS YOU FALL IN.

★